BYRDMAN'S TRAVELS

A Fly-by-Night Affair: We'll Take You for a Ride

by

B. Charles Stuter

The contents of this work, including, but not limited to, the accuracy of events, people, and places depicted; opinions expressed; permission to use previously published materials included; and any advice given or actions advocated are solely the responsibility of the author, who assumes all liability for said work and indemnifies the publisher against any claims stemming from publication of the work.

All Rights Reserved
Copyright © 2016 by B. Charles Stuter

No part of this book may be reproduced or transmitted, downloaded, distributed, reverse engineered, or stored in or introduced into any information storage and retrieval system, in any form or by any means, including photocopying and recording, whether electronic or mechanical, now known or hereinafter invented without permission in writing from the publisher.

Dorrance Publishing Co
585 Alpha Drive
Suite 103
Pittsburgh, PA 15238
Visit our website at *www.dorrancebookstore.com*

ISBN: 978-1-4809-3158-9
eISBN: 978-1-4809-3135-0

This is dedicated to Bob Mosher, my best friend.

Hi! Welcome to Byrdman's Travels. Please, come in, and have a seat. Make yourself comfortable. Yes, all we have are pillows and cushions. Sorry about that. If you want food or drink, the milk and cookies are over on that table.

What is this place? It's just a place in which to hang out and to share stories with people. Yes, that's all. What about me? Well, I was raised in a small farming community in central Pennsylvania. This was during the sixties, and everyone in my class wanted to go to college to be a scientist. Sputnik had its effect on all of us. We were all Republicans, but we still liked President Kennedy. I went to West Virginia University, got my degree in mechanical engineering, and I knew from graduation day that I never wanted to be an engineer. I was accepted into Advanced ROTC, and, upon graduation, I was commissioned into the United States Air Force as a Second Lieutenant. I wanted to fly! That's what birds do!

My first duty assignment was to Sheppard Air Force Base in Wichita Falls, Texas. I flunked out of pilot training. I still wanted to fly so I was assigned to Mather AFB, Sacramento, California. I graduated from there as a B-52 navigator. I drove up to Fairchild AFB in Spokane, Washington, to an empty base. The entire B-52 Wing was sitting on Guam flying combat missions over Vietnam.

During the next twenty years, I travelled to Guam, Thailand, Spain, Germany, and North Dakota. I retired back to Spokane for two reasons: The jobs were better, and my wife was from Idaho. Now, at forty-two, what did I want to do with my life? I applied to and attended International Air Academy. I was hired by Horizon Air and based in Spokane, Washington.

"Is Byrd your real name?" they ask.

"Yes," I reply.

"That's a great name for someone working for the airlines."

"Would you like to hear the rest of the story?"

"Please."

"I'm retired military, and I flew in the Air Force, too!"

TICKET COUNTER

BRAIN BOXES
When you come to the airport, you notice large containers beside each entry door. These are not trash cans. They are "brain boxes." It seems some airline customers deposit their brains and their common sense into these receptacles because once inside, they are lost as to where they need to go, when they need to go, how they need to go, and what time they need to go.

JOE
A young man came to me and asked when my next flight from Montana arrived. I asked him from what city. He didn't know. I asked him at what time the flight was to arrive. He didn't know. I asked him what the last name of his friend was. Again, he didn't know.

I said, "I can't help you."

He replied, "Can't you look it up in the computer? His name's Joe!"

THE BLONDE
A blonde female came to Mary Shea who was working beside me.

Mary Shea asked, "What time are you leaving?"

"Five thirty."

"It's ten minutes to six. You missed your flight."

"I know I'm supposed to leave at five thirty."

"It's ten minutes to six. You missed your flight."

"Well, we had the rental car, and I'm supposed to leave at five thirty."

Mary stated: "Did you turn your clock ahead one hour last night?" (It was Spring Daylight Savings Time changeover.)

"No. We had the rental car in Coeur d'Alene, and I thought it was their responsibility to do that!" Duh!

Baggage

A woman came to me at the counter and handed me the tickets for herself and her husband. He was carrying their luggage from the car. I checked both of them in for their flight, and I asked the woman, "Do you have any baggage to check?"

She replied, "Just my husband!"

No Teeth

A woman and her young son came to check in. The boy was very small, and his front teeth were missing. As I leaned over to place the bag tag onto the suitcase, the boy asked, "Whath your name?"

"My name is Byrd."

He looked at me with a funny face and said, "Byrd? You don't look like a bird. You don't have any featherths!"

Triple Bogey

A couple was flying to Las Vegas. Each had a suitcase, and the man had a set of golf clubs. As I tagged the golf bag, the man stated emphatically, "You can lose my wife, but don't lose my golf clubs!"

The wife's face slowly turned pink, and by the time they had left the ticket counter, it was scarlet. I'm surprised she didn't just pull out a three iron and wrap it around her husband's neck!

Las Vegas

Another couple was flying to Las Vegas. I was talking with the husband. "Don't forget to bring your shirt back with you," I said.

"What?" His wife began to giggle.

"Don't forget to bring your shirt back with you."

"What?" His wife began to laugh.

"Don't forget to bring your shirt back with you."

"Why wouldn't I bring my shirt back with me? I'm not going to fly back nude!"

"You don't want to lose your shirt in Las Vegas!" I said.

He slapped the palm of his hand against his forehead and said, "I never saw that one coming!" His wife grabbed him by the arm and whispered, "Come along dear," and off they went!

Pizza

I checked in a college girl and asked her if she had a funny story. She said that she had a foreign exchange student from Italy in one of her classes. One day she took him to eat at Pizza Pipeline. Hey, a poor college kid will eat anything! The Italian boy liked the pizza so much that he went around to all his friends telling them to eat at Peetza Pippa Lee Nee!

Geography

A group of young people came to the counter to check in. Most of the group went to the girl beside me. I asked the man in front of me what his destination was.

"Tacoma," he said.

"We don't fly to Tacoma. We fly to Seattle."

"I'm going to Tacoma."

"We don't fly to Tacoma. We fly to Seattle."

His friends overheard this conversation and said, "Hey, Joe. It's the same airport!"

Joe turned to me and said, "You can tell that I don't get out very much."

In my mind, I thought, "I can tell you're not a geography major either!"

Tragedy

Two women came to check in. They had driven four hours from Oroville in north-central Washington. Their nephew was in the Intensive Care Unit in a Denver hospital. He had been in a car accident. I called the hospital to confirm this. The women had no reservation and had a limited amount of cash for which to pay for the flights. I made a roundtrip reservation and priced it for them; it was more than they could afford.

Throwing out procedure, I made a three-week, made-in-advance, round-trip reservation for them so they could be afforded the cheapest price. They were going to fly from Spokane to Seattle to Los Angeles on Alaska Airlines and then to Denver on Morris Air. I checked their luggage free of charge, gave them their boarding passes, and sent them to the gate. After their plane took off, the hospital called and said the nephew had died. The two women were now going to a funeral.

THE KAYAK
A man brought a large rubber bag and a small kayak to check in. He was flying to Anchorage. He set the kayak beside me on the scale and the bag next to Shanna. She got his boarding pass and ran the bag tags. I stepped across the kayak to take the bag tags, but I tripped. I fell head-over-heels forward and my cheek bounced off her buttocks. I fell flat onto my face on the floor. I got up, brushed myself off, and tagged the bag and the kayak. Shanna threw the bag onto the moving carousel while I carried the kayak to the oversized item door.

When I returned, the man had left, and grinning from ear to ear, Shanna said to me: "Byrd, if you wanted to kiss my ass all you had to do was ask!"

AGE I
An elderly woman came to check in. I asked her for her driver's license.

She replied, "Don't look at the picture. It's really ugly."

I said, "We never look at the picture; we just look at the age!"

"What do you mean, you look at the age! Nobody knows my age!"

"It was just a joke."

"Well, it better be because nobody knows my age!"

That's with the woman's driver's license staring me in the face with her date of birth!

AGE II
A few weeks later, a young girl and her mother came to check in. The young girl was flying. I asked her for her driver's license.

She said, "Don't look at the picture. It's really ugly!"

I repeated the story of the elderly woman. When I was finished, the mother said, "At least you didn't ask for the age and the weight both!"

I looked at the mother and stated, "Ma'am, I might be a man, but I'm old enough to know that some things are just not to be discussed!"

SAN DIEGO
A couple was flying to San Diego. Each had a suitcase. I told them that one bag was going to Sea World and the other bag was going to the San Diego Zoo. Both laughed.

A few days later, another couple was doing the same thing, and each had their own suitcases. I told them, as well, that one bag was going to the zoo, and the other bag was going to Sea World. Both times the wife asserted: "His is going to the zoo!"

Graveyard Humor

A woman came to check in for her flight. She was very crippled. After I had given the boarding pass to her, I asked if she needed any assistance.

She replied, "No, I'm going to visit my daughter and my granddaughter. If I fall over while I'm there, my daughter can just hang me from the ceiling of the front porch. When all the skin falls off, with all the metal I have inside my body, I'll just turn into a wind chime!"

Selfish

My female coworkers took ballpoint pens and made them into rose-topped stems. One day a woman came to check in. She used the rose-topped pen to fill out a name tag. Then she asked, "May I have this pen?"

"No," I replied.

Forty-five seconds of total silence ensued. Then the woman retorted, "Selfish!"

Put Down

Steve and I were working beside each other. Business was extremely slow, and we were trying to keep awake. I was chatting with him at his computer station. A woman in her fifties came to the counter.

Steve asked, "May I help you?"

"I need to check in," the woman exclaimed.

"What time are you leaving?"

"I want him to check me in (pointing to me)."

"I can help you," said Steve.

"No, I want him to check me in (again pointing to me)."

"Thank you," I replied.

"But I don't have a computer, and besides, Steve is younger than me."

Looking directly at Steve, she stated, "You might be younger, but he's better looking!"

Disneyland

In 1998 I worked one entire summer from 3:30 A.M. until noon. I am not a morning person! To everyone that I checked in, I would ask: "Well, are you going to Disneyland today?" The answer was always no.

The next schedule change I bid my usual afternoon shift. A woman was standing alone, and I called her over to check her in. Automatically, I asked: "Well, are you going to Disneyland today?"

She replied, "No....we own it!" Her last name was Disney, and she had an Anaheim, California, address!

After she left, I looked at Google on the Internet. I typed in Walt Disney's wife. I learned that he had been born in Spaulding, Idaho, and had grown up in Lapwai. In September 2013, I told this story to one of my customers.

She responded, "You won't believe this, but my grandmother grew up in Lapwai, and her next door neighbor was the future Mrs. Walt Disney!" It truly is a small world!

Seven Pounds

A German woman and her son were returning to Germany. They had three, small duffel bags and one, large, heavy suitcase. I weighed the suitcase, and it was seven pounds over the required limit.

I said, "Is it possible to take seven pounds of items out of this suitcase and put them inside the other bags? Otherwise, I will have to charge you the overweight fee." Overweight bags traveling internationally are very expensive.

"Do you accept American Express?" she replied. One $125 later, I sent the bag back to Onload. For seven pounds!

Oops

A non-revenue (airline employee) couple was flying up to Alaska. They had thirteen cardboard boxes to check. At that time, each passenger was allowed three checked bags free of charge. I had to charge them for seven boxes—a total of $300!

As the last box went through the opening into Onload, the wife stated to me, "Maybe we should have sent them Federal Express!"

B-52 Strike

A man my age came to check in for his flight. I asked for his identification.

He said, "It's military."

I said, "That's okay. I'm retired military myself. It's government issued, and it's legal."

"Were you in the Army? he asked.

"No, I was a B-52 navigator in the Air Force."

"You guys almost bombed my head one night in Vietnam."

"I'm sorry," I said.

"Oh, no, it's okay. Our platoon was surrounded by Viet Cong, and we called in a B-52 strike. If it weren't for that, I wouldn't be talking with you today."

Thank You

I checked in a man one day with the last name of Nuremberger. I asked him if his family had originally come from Nuremberg (Nurnberg), Germany. He said that they had. I told him that my grandmother had given a book to me in high school titled The Toys of Nuremberg. I wrote down the title of the book with its author and gave it to him.

About six months later, I worked for a coworker on my day off. A family checked in with the girl working beside me. An elderly woman and a young girl left the group and walked over to where I was working.

The woman began to speak; she had a German accent. "Are you the gentleman who recommended the book *The Toys of Nuremberg*?"

"Yes, I am."

"I want to thank you," she said. "I went online on the computer and found a first edition of the book, and I bought it for my granddaughter here for Christmas."

Jerry

My friend, Jerry, used to work for Alaska Airlines. I know this story is true because I heard of it through two primary participants. Jerry was working the ticket counter. A customer was screaming at him for the usual reasons: The inbound flight was late; he didn't have an exit row aisle seat; and why couldn't Jerry do something about it?

A man standing behind the screamer tapped him on the shoulder and stated: "Why are you screaming at the ticket agent? It isn't his fault that the flight is late."

The screamer turned to the man and screamed in response, "Do I know you?"

"No," the second man stated.

"Then shut the f*** up!"

The screamer left for the gate, and Jerry checked in the second man.

That man walked to the gate and found the same scenario: The screamer was berating the gate agent for the exact same things he did at the ticket counter. The plane finally arrived, and both men boarded and flew to Seattle. The second man made his connection to Los Angeles and, upon arrival, went to his office to set up a business meeting to review bids for building contracts in the city. Guess who walked into the room? Exactly: the screamer with his boss!

The moderator asked the boss, "Does this man work for you?"

The boss replied that the screamer did work for him. The moderator told the boss to put away his building bids and the two were to leave the room. The bids were not even going to be reviewed. The boss asked why, and the moderator told him what the screamer had done in Spokane. The moderator again asked the boss if the screamer still worked for him.

The boss turned in his chair and told the screamer to "leave the room. You no longer have a job."

After the screamer left, the moderator politely asked the boss to reopen his bids because they were to be reviewed. After the meeting ended, the moderator left the room and walked out into the hallway only to find the screamer waiting for him. The screamer began another tirade. The moderator politely made this statement:

"Don't even think of it! I am a retired Marine Drill Sergeant, and with one hand behind my back, I can kill you. I suggest you just walk away from here and find a new job."

Dial-A-Plane

We had had several cancelled flights that day, and the ticket counter was packed with customers whose flights were being rebooked. I was helping a man trying to get to Southern California.

I kept looking for available flights when the frustrated guy said, "Can't you get another airplane in here to fly all these people out?"

"No, sir, I can't," I said.

"Well can't you just call someone on the telephone and order a new plane?"

"No, sir, I can't do that either." I almost asked the guy for the telephone number for Dial-A-Plane because I certainly didn't know it!

CAR RENTALS

Here in Spokane, our ticket counter is at least a quarter mile from the car rentals. They are literally at the other end of the airport. One day a gentleman left security from his inbound flight and approached me at the counter. He asked the following question: "How much is a one-way ticket to the car rentals?"

MEXICO

One day two females came to me. Both were covered in tattoos. One woman was flying to Cabo San Lucas, Mexico. I typed in the passport information, checked her bag, and gave her the boarding pass.

"You're really nice," she said.

"Thank you," I replied.

"Do you want to come with me?" she asked.

"Well, I did spend three years in Spain, and I can speak a little Spanish."

"Great," said the woman. We can go dancing, takes some shots (of tequila), go to the beach, and get naked!"

Not in my lifetime I thought to myself!

A WASTE OF PAPER

A sports team from one of the local universities came to check in. There were twenty-five students, all in the same reservation. One student had changed something, and I was forced to charge him a $25 change fee. I hit the "Enter" key, and twenty-five change fees printed! I had to delete twenty-four of them.

The next day, Holly came to me, showed me all the deleted coupons, and sternly reprimanded me by stating, "Next time, Byrd, use name select!"

COOKIES, COOKIES EVERYWHERE

A girl from the Boise ticket counter called one day. She said that she had sold a Mr. Hall a ticket to Spokane. The agent said that Mr. Hall paid in cash, but she failed to collect the money. The girl asked if I could page Mr. Hall over the intercom and try to collect the money owed. I told her that I would try.

I made the page, and almost instantaneously Mr. Hall appeared in front of me. I explained the situation to him. He showed me his ticket receipt, and "cash" was written as the form of payment.

Mr. Hall said, "I paid her in cash. I know how much money I have in my wallet." He opened his wallet, counted the money, and said, "Damn! I did forget to give her the money!" Mr. Hall immediately paid me the correct amount owed—in cash.

I called the girl in Boise, and I told her I had collected the money. She told me that she had already been updating her resume—in case she had gotten fired.

She asked, "What about the money? My till is wrong, and so is yours. How will we fix that?" I told her that I would add an overage to my account, and she should add a shortage to her account. General Accounting would receive these both, and everything would become "a wash."

The agent profusely thanked me for my help, and she asked if there were anything that she could do for me. Anything! I told her that she could make me some homemade chocolate chip cookies and send them via company mail to Spokane.

The next day, a tin of cookies arrived for me from Boise. It contained five dozen homemade chocolate chip cookies! The girl must have spent all night cooking over a hot oven to thank me!

Peanuts

A man asked me what type of food was served on the airplane. I said that we served free wine and beer, as well as snacks from different companies throughout the Pacific Northwest.

"What about peanuts? he asked.

I said that we served peanuts, too. "Don't eat the peanuts," I said.

"Why not?" the man asked.

"It's my next pay raise!"

Three Men Named Max

A female passenger told this story to me: Her daughter was dating a man in Denver named Max. The relationship was on again, off again. The man could not decide if he wanted to marry this girl.

One day the girl was driving on the freeway, south of Seattle, when her tire blew out. A good Samaritan stopped and changed her tire. His name was

Max. This man gave the girl his telephone number and said to call him if she ever wanted to go out for a beer together. The girl said that she would like that. The Max in Denver still would not commit, so the girl called the telephone number the second Max had given her. The telephone was answered by a man named Max. The girl stated that she wanted to share a beer together in appreciation for his changing her flat tire. The man replied, "Yes, my name is Max, but I never changed a flat tire for you!"

To make a longer story shorter, the girl dumped the Max in Denver for non-committal, had no idea what the second Max's real telephone number was, and ended by marrying the third Max!!

Blonde Mice

The Alaska agents used to have their ticket counter right beside ours. They got off work before us, too. One evening their door opened and nine agents in queue, led by a blonde girl, walked out toward the street.

I looked at them and said to the girl beside me, "Look. It's the blonde leading the blind!"

Santa Ana

Whenever I check in passengers flying to Santa Ana, California, I tell them that they must check three bags: one for Santa Ana, one for Orange County, and one for John Wayne. It's the only airport in the world with three names!

One day I told this to a woman, and she said, "No, you must check four bags: an extra one in which to hold all the silicon. If my neighborhood in Beverly Hills ever burned down, all that silicon around me would melt!"

Rocks

One day I checked in a man who had a very small duffel bag. I put the bag tag around the handle and went to lift it. I almost pulled my arm from my socket; it was so heavy!

"What do you have in there? Rocks?"

"Yes," the man replied. "I'm a geologist!"

Wrong

A woman checked in with a preprinted boarding pass. "May I see it? I asked. She gave me seven copies of the boarding pass. "Hmm. Seven copies. This looks to me like operator error!" I stated.

"It is not operator error. I didn't push the button that many times!"

I thought to myself: Then how the hell did you end up with seven copies of the same thing?

Identification

A middle-aged woman was checking in. "May I see if you're old enough to fly by yourself (meaning may I see your ID)? My mother keeps telling me that she's thirty-nine, and you're a whole lot younger than my mother!"

The woman gave her driver's license to me and said, "Oh, you're good!"

I gave the woman her boarding pass and said, "You're leaving from Gate 23. If you can't remember the gate, just remember your age!"

"Oh, you're really good," she said.

"Are you married?" she asked.

"Yes."

"Damn!"

Cruise

The day of the week was Saturday. A couple came to check in. The wife handed me the tickets, and I tried to give them their boarding passes. I wasn't able. On further inspection, I noticed the flight numbers were for Friday, the day before. I mentioned this to the wife and continued to change the reservation.

The wife thought a bit and stated, "I wonder if we missed our cruise, too?" She opened her purse and looked at the itinerary. "We missed it," she said. "Give me back the tickets."

The husband never said a word. He just turned around and headed for the door. It seems the couple was to fly to Los Angeles on Friday and catch the cruise ship on Saturday. I'm really glad that I didn't hear the argument in the car. It was the couple's yearly vacation, and the cruise was non-refundable.

Dog

When we still used real tickets, a man approached me at the ticket counter. I asked him when he was flying and requested his ticket. He handed me the ticket in a Ziploc bag! The ticket inside was in pieces and parts. I looked at the ticket and then at the man, and I stated, "If you asked me, it looks like the dog ate it."

The man replied, "As a matter of fact, he did!"

I dumped all the ticket pieces onto the counter, got out the Scotch tape, and taped it all together. The ticket number was intact, so the ticket was still valid. The man went to the gate, gave his ticket to the agent there, and that is how it was sent into accounting—all taped together!

Simple

A man came to the ticket counter and asked the following question: "On the arrival board over there, there is a 'p' after the times. What does that mean?"

I replied, "It's for A.M. and P.M."

"It's that simple?" he asked.

"Yes," I replied, "it's that simple!"

DEPARTURE GATE

FIRST CLASS
A woman came to me and asked if I could change her seat. After that was done, I asked, "Is there anything else I can do for you?"

She said, "Do you have first class available for my connection?"

I looked at availability of seats and noticed one first-seat seat was available on her connection flight. I rebooked her from coach to first class without telling her. "Here," I said. She took the boarding pass, turned around, and began to walk away from the podium.

She looked down at the boarding pass, saw what I had done, looked at the audience while raising her arms into the air, and screamed, "He did it!"

BILLINGS
A guy approached my podium and slammed his tickets onto the counter. "I want the filet mignon flight to Billings," he said adamantly.

"I'm sorry, sir, but all we have today is steak and lobster," I responded.

"And I don't suppose you have first class, either?"

"No, we don't need first class because we're a first-class airline!"

"That's what the girl in Portland said, and when I reached over to read her name tag, she told me where to go!"

"Well, she probably told you to go to Helena!"

"As a matter of fact she did, but I want to go to Billings."

"Why don't you fly to Helena as the girl in Portland suggested, rent a car, drive to Billings, and see the great state of Montana?"

"That's a great idea, but I just want to go to Billings."

"Gate 23," I pointed to him.

He picked up his tickets and walked away!

Byrd and the Chicks

Missy, Tammy, Kara, and I worked all summer together. They were all single, all beautiful, and all less than twenty-one years of age. One day, Missy came to me and giggled, "We should give ourselves a name since we're going to be working together all summer."

"What kind of name?" I asked.

"You know, like a rock group or something."

She left to board a flight. An hour later, Missy returned and suggested, "I have our name. It's going to be Byrd and the Chicks!"

"That's cool," I responded. All summer we were Byrd and the Chicks. Years later, all the male Passenger Service Agents (PSA) either quit or transferred from Spokane, and I was the lone PSA agent inside. It was, literally, Byrd and all the Chicks!

Fast

The inbound flight was running late. The ramp lead said that when the last person came off the plane, the first person was to board. Throwing procedure out the window, I made the following boarding announcement: "Ladies and gentlemen, because this flight arrived so late, we are dispensing with normal boarding procedures. We are going to pretend we are Southwest Airlines today! As everyone passes by me here at the podium, just give your seat number only."

I had previously printed the passenger name list with every person's name and seat number on it. The passengers filed out toward the ramp, giving only their seat number as they walked by me. By the time the last person was onboard, I had entered everyone's name into the computer. We made up ten minutes of ground time just by doing this.

Beverly

Beverly was a black girl who worked as a passenger service agent for Southwest Airlines. One evening we were walking out to the employee parking lot together.

"How's it going, Beverly?" I asked.

"Byrd," she responded, "Southwest has me jumpin'. As a new supervisor, they just have me jumpin'. They have me closing the ticket counter in the evening and opening the ticket counter in the morning. They have me doing almost everything! They just have me jumpin'. Does Horizon have you jumpin', Byrd?"

"No," I said, "everybody knows white men can't jump!" She laughed so hard she cried!

My Airline

The Missoula station called us one day. They said that on their last flight to Spokane, a passenger was on board who they felt was intoxicated. We advised our supervisor, and he met the aircraft after it was parked. Yes, the supervisor determined that the passenger was indeed intoxicated. Dave told him that he would not be continuing his flight to Seattle for another three hours.

"Why?" asked the man.

"You're intoxicated. Due to that, you can't fly on my airline."

"It's not your airline," slurred the man.

"It is my airline," responded the supervisor, "And you can't get on this next flight to Seattle."

"How is it your airline? You don't own it," said the man.

"As a matter of fact, I do. I own Alaska Airlines stock in my 401(k) plan, and because of that, I own part of the airline. Therefore, it's my airline, and you can't fly on it!" The man left three hours later.

Remembering

I sent a copy of these stories to Dave, an Alaska pilot who commutes a lot to Seattle out of Spokane. When I saw him one day at the gate, I asked him if he liked these stories. He stated that he loved the stories. He just couldn't believe that I could remember so much detail. He said I must have had a pile of notes to type. When I told him that it only took two weeks to type and that everything was from memory, Dave responded: "Memory? I can't remember anything anymore. My mind is beer shot!"

California Girl

I had just finished boarding a flight. I printed the paperwork and carried it out to the airplane to give to the flight attendant. Upon entering the plane, the flight attendant asked, "Are you full?"

"Full", I replied. "We are totally—I mean totally—full!"

She walked down the aisle, did the count, and returned to me standing at the door. "You are totally correct!" she stated.

BAGGAGE SERVICE

Blue Bag

A passenger entered the office and said his suitcase wasn't on the carousel. I typed the entire lost baggage report, but I didn't "end" it because there was one black bag left on the carousel. I went over, retrieved the bag, and looked at the luggage tag. "This is your bag. It has your name on it," I said.

"That isn't my bag," was the reply. "My bag is blue."

I opened the upper compartment of the bag, and the man stated, "What's my stuff doing it that bag? My bag is blue."

"It's your bag," I replied.

"No it's not," he retorted. "My bag is blue."

I then opened the main part of the bag and found a medicine bottle with the passenger's name on it. "This is your bag. It has your name on two items."

Exasperated, the passenger said, "Well, it was blue when I left!"

What Are You Studying?

Holly was working with me this night. A flight's luggage was being offloaded onto the carousel. A ramp agent brought in a plastic bag through the back door. Inside was a smashed, antique table.

Soon a college student came into the office looking for his table which he had bought in Seattle that day for $300. "You mean this one?" I asked.

"Yes," he said, "that one. What happened to it?"

"This is how the ramp agents found it on the airplane."

"Then you'll have to compensate me for it."

"I'm sorry, sir, but heirlooms and antiques are not covered under the baggage agreement."

"I'm not leaving this office until I get a new table or compensation."

"It's eleven o'clock at night! It's impossible to get you a table. And besides, we don't cover antiques."

"Then I'll get my own compensation," he said.

"How do you expect to do that?" I asked.

"I'll just take this bag sitting here!"

"That would be stealing. If you take it, we'll have to call the airport police."

"Go ahead," he said.

Holly picked up the telephone receiver and began to dial the number for the police department. The guy put down the bag and left the office, walking outside to the curb. The police arrived, and Holly explained to them what had happened. The police went to look for the guy.

Ten minutes later, the police returned and said they had found him across the street. They had asked him for his driver's license, but he refused, saying, "Legally, l don't have to give it to you."

"That's true," stated one of the officers, "and legally, we can arrest you for not producing it, as well!"

The police stated that he was a Gonzaga University law student! I told Holly that I would write up this report in his PNR.

She said, "No need. While he was talking, I was typing everything that he said into it already!" Would anyone ever want this guy as their lawyer?

FLIRTING

An elderly lady flew into Spokane, and her suitcase was delayed. Two female friends were there to drive her home. I began to type the delayed baggage report. I kept asking her the usual questions with some other conversation, as well.

The next thing I know, she says, "I think this man is flirting with me!"

"As a matter of fact, I am," I replied.

"Well," she snorted, "I'm not going to talk to you again!" She then turned her back to me.

"That's okay," I said. "I already have your name, address, and telephone number!"

With that her girlfriends gave her the "raspberries": "Sadie, you're such a prude, and here you are giving all your vital statistics to every good looking guy who comes along!"

All I could do was laugh. After all, her back was turned to me!

Responsibility

A guy is missing his suitcase. As I'm doing the claim, I ask him what something specific is inside the bag.

He says, "My car keys. You'll have to rent me a cab so I can get home to Coeur d'Alene."

"I can't do that, sir. You're the one who packed your suitcase."

"Then you'll have to rent me a car so I can get home."

"I can't do that, either. You're the one who packed your suitcase."

"Well, don't blame me!" he yelled. "You're the one who lost my suitcase!"

Too Young

I typed a missing bag report. The man in front of me began to tell me a story. He abruptly stopped and said, "You're too young to know about what I'm talking."

"How old do you think I am?" I responded.

He looked at me and said, "Forty-eight."

"Well, you've missed it by ten years!"

"You mean to tell me you're fifty-eight years old?"

"Yes."

"May I ask you a personal question?"

"Yes."

"How do you stay so young-looking?"

"Well," I stated, "I work with all these beautiful women, and all that beauty rubs off on me!"

You know what he didn't ask? How it rubbed off!

BS

BS does not stand for Byrd Stuter. It does not stand for Baggage Service. It certainly does not stand for Bart Simpson; nor does is stand for bulls****. It stands for Beyond Sanity because anyone would have to be Beyond Sanity to work in the Spokane baggage service office as many years as I have and still be able to talk and converse politely!

Short Circuit

It was Christmas time. Melodee, our secretary, came into the office. I was taking a baggage claim. Realizing that it would be awhile before I would be finished,

Melodee quietly walked up beside me and whispered "Merry Christmas" into my ear, kissed me on the cheek, and departed.

My mind went completely blank! Her kiss totally crossed my brainwaves! I couldn't remember what I was supposed to do next. I had to start the bag claim over from scratch!

Mr. Graham

Mr. Graham was missing his golf clubs. He had flown that day from Guam to Seattle on Northwest Airlines, and from Seattle to Spokane on Horizon Air. I began to type the claim. He was furious! Every other word began with the letter "F." "F*** this" and "F*** that" was all he seemed to say. He left.

A little over an hour later, he returned. He was still angry. His language hadn't changed at all. He asked the whereabouts of his golf clubs, and I said that I didn't know. He left again.

Mr. Graham returned to the airport four times that night trying to find out where his golf clubs were! As he left the office for the final time, he spat, "You're so incompetent that you should be working for McDonalds!"

When I finally retire from this job and if I ever do work for McDonalds and I see Mr. Graham again, he'll be lucky to get a six-month-old bun!

A New York City Minute

My friend, Bob, worked for Alaska Airlines in Spokane. We worked the same shifts, same times, and had same days off. One night a woman who lived in New York City was missing her suitcase, and Bob did the delay report. When he finished, he handed the woman the receipt and told her that when her bag arrived, it would be delivered to the local address.

"You know I can't leave the airport without my suitcase," the woman said.

"Why not?" Bob asked.

"Because my whole face is in my suitcase!"

"We'll deliver your bag."

"No, you don't understand. My face is in my suitcase, and I can't leave the airport without it!"

"We'll deliver your bag," Bob kept repeating.

"You don't understand; you're a man."

"Would you like an overnight kit?"

"What's that?"

"It's a kit with a comb, toothbrush, toothpaste, and an inflatable nightgown in it."

"Inflatable nightgown? What's that?"

"It's a nightgown that you open and just slip into."

"It'd probably be too small for me anyway!"

If you're ever given an airline overnight kit, please don't look for the inflatable nightgown; it doesn't exist! Bob just threw that into the conversation, but the woman was so headstrong and angry, she didn't even know the difference!

Compensation

A guy was missing his bag. Bob was doing the claim. The guy kept ranting and raving while Bob typed.

"This is the third time this month that I've flown Alaska Airlines, and it is the third time this month that you guys have lost my bag. I'm never going to fly Alaska Airlines again!"

Bob gave the guy his receipt. The man walked out of the office about ten feet, turned on his heel, and walked right back into the office. "What about compensation?" the man asked.

"What about compensation?" Bob replied.

"It's the third time this month that you guys have lost my bag, and I want some compensation."

"We can't do that," Bob stated.

"Then I want a free first-class, round-trip ticket."

"We can't do that, either."

"Why not?"

"Because you just said that you were never flying Alaska Airlines again!"

Mister Wick

Mister Wick lost his box of fish. I completed the claim, told him that I would call him as soon as it arrived, and have it delivered. A few hours later, the fish box arrived. I called Mr. Wick and said I would have it delivered by our baggage delivery service. I got really busy since I was alone in the office.

Hours later Mr. Wick called wanting to know about the fish. I explained to him that I was really busy, and, at that time, the only way for me to get it delivered was by taxicab. That would be after midnight. He was not happy.

He ranted about the fish thawing out, about the cost of shipping the fish, and about my inadequacy as a customer service agent.

I said, "If you want your fish tonight, you'll have to come out to the airport and pick it up yourself."

An hour later, Mr. Wick came into my office with a young college girl hanging on each arm. I gave him the box of fish. He kept ranting about the fish thawing out and my poor customer service. Bob, who worked next door, came over and told him to leave. Mr. Wick moved toward me aggressively.

Bob said, "I'm going to count to ten, and then I'm going to call the airport police. One—ten!" and he began to dial the telephone.

Mr. Wick turned around, threw the fish box over his shoulder, and left with the girls, ranting the entire time.

Months later I visited Bob's house. He wanted me to watch a movie entitled *A Little Box of Moonlight*. It concerned a stranded business man in the outback of Arkansas. He met all types of people. The bad guys in the movie were a pair of brothers who drove a white panel truck. On the side of the truck was painted "Wick Brothers!" It must run in the family, even in Hollywood!

SALMON GOLF BAG

A guy flew in from Anchorage. He checked a bag and a set of golf clubs. The golf clubs weren't here. I typed the claim, give him the receipt, and told him we'd deliver them when it arrived.

The man asked, "What about the salmon?"

"What salmon?" I said.

"The salmon I put inside the golf bag!"

"You put a salmon inside your golf bag?"

"Yes."

"Did you tell anyone that you put a salmon inside your golf bag?"

"No."

"Well then, we'll be able to find it in about three days!"

PINK BLANKEE

A week later, another guy flew from Anchorage, and he, too, was missing his golf clubs. His best friend was there to take him home. I typed the claim.

Remembering the salmon, I asked the man, "Is there anything else inside your golf bag besides golf clubs?"

"My pink blankee!" the guy replied.

The friend asked, "You have a pink blankee inside your golf bag?"

"Yes, but don't tell anyone."

"Too late!" the friend responded happily.

Annika Sorenstam

A man was missing his golf bag. I was typing the claim. This was when Annika Sorenstam played in the Masters golf tournament. He asked me if I played golf. I said I did not. He said, "You should. Do you know what the letters g-o-l-f mean?" I said that I did not. The man exclaimed, "Gentleman Only; Ladies Forbidden!" He was totally serious, too.

Nightmare On Elm Street

Cortney and I were working together. A couple flew in from Mexico. When the man lifted his suitcase off the carousel, liquid was dripping from the bottom. He set the suitcase on the floor, opened it, and stuck his hand inside a brown paper bag. The bag contained an unwrapped bottle of tequila, totally smashed. The man pulled his hand from the paper bag, and it dripped blood. Did he go to the bathroom to clean it? No, he walked into the baggage office and began to slam his shredded hand onto our counter, demanding that we buy him a new bottle of tequila. We told him that since the bottle was unwrapped, the baggage agreement did not cover that. He kept slamming his fist onto the counter, all the while profusely swearing. We had blood everywhere: on the counter, on the computers, on the front glass window, and even on the telephones.

The man finally ended his tantrum and walked out to the street. I immediately found a box of large towels and began spreading them everywhere. Cortney found disinfectant and began spraying everything. When we completed cleaning (it took over a half hour), we called airport janitorial service to clean the line of blood from our front door to the curb. There was only one way we could calm ourselves: eat chocolate! We hit the Reese's Cups pretty hard!

You're Despicable

A woman using a wheelchair was flying from Spokane to Ontario, California, through Seattle. She missed her early afternoon flight. My supervisor rebooked her for a flight that evening which would get her into Ontario before midnight.

When it came time to board the later flight, she felt ill and did not board. My supervisor rebooked her for the following morning. He called me in baggage service and advised me to get a hotel voucher, as well as a breakfast voucher ready when the woman came down to see me. The woman came down to me to pick up the vouchers.

As I was giving her the coupons, she asked, "Do I get any compensation for this?"

"No, ma'am, you don't."

"Why won't I get any compensation for my delay?" she asked.

First of all," I replied, "you're not entitled to compensation, and secondly, we're giving you a free hotel for the night and a free breakfast, as well."

"No compensation, and I'm in a wheelchair, too. You're despicable!"

I almost wanted to tear those coupons in half.

Customer Service

A man's suitcase had not arrived. I was typing the report. The man was screaming at me at the top of his lungs: "I want your name; I want your badge number; I want your supervisor's name; I want your station manager's name; and I'm going to have your job!"

I only smiled. I thought: "Great! Then you can be on this side of the counter, and I can be on that side of the counter, screaming and swearing at the tops of my lungs, and you can't do a damned thing about it because you have to provide superior customer service!"

Bag Swap

A customer picked up the wrong bag one day. This was Sunday afternoon. He was to spend the next week in Sandpoint, Idaho. I called him innumerable times that day and the next asking him to return the other bag and to pick up his bag in our office. The guy stated that he was flying out on Saturday to return to Billings. I finally told the guy that if he didn't return the bag, we would call the local police to obtain it because this was a form of stealing.

"Go ahead," he said.

I told my supervisor this, and she called the guy. She said that he needed to return the bag the next day. The guy said that he would return the bag on Saturday when he was flying out.

My supervisor said, "You're not flying out of Spokane on Saturday."

"Why not?" he asked in surprise.

"Because I just cancelled your reservation!" she replied.

The guy sheepishly returned the bag the next day and retrieved his.

CARDIAC ARREST

On a Tuesday, a ramp agent brought in a medium-sized box of Godiva Chocolates that had been left onboard an airplane. Nobody came into the office all week long to claim it.

That Saturday, Michelle, an Alaska agent, and I were working together. We had three hours until the next aircraft arrival.

Michelle said, "I'm making a McDonalds run." She returned later with many medium-sized boxes of French fries. We got as many PSA people together in our office and "pigged out" with McDonald's French fries for the main course, and Godiva chocolates for dessert.

PINK DRESS

A college student who had just flown from Asia was missing his suitcase. As I was typing the report, I asked him for something specific inside in which to identify his bag. The boy said, "My pink dress. It's the only one I have!"

I typed that exactly into the report!

LEGS

Our baggage office used to sit beside the Southwest Airlines baggage office. It's where Delta is now. I left the podium there and walked past Southwest's office. Just as I did, Kathy, an Alaska agent, rounded the corner by the Southwest ticket counter. It was summer, and she was wearing her white shirt with shorts. I stopped dead in my tracks and watched Kathy walk the entire way down to where I stood.

"Why did you stop walking, Byrd?" she asked.

I replied, "I always stop for a pair of good-looking legs!"

MATCHMAKER

I used to work with Margaret. She was very young, very pretty, and very single. One day, she began to discuss our Cargo supervisor, Todd. This continued for several days. When I saw Todd later in the month, I told him about Margaret's conversations with me.

"I think she likes you. Why don't you ask her out?" I said. He did. They fell in love. They got married. They now have three children. Voila!

Australia

Bill Gadau used to work in the Ops office. One day I walked in and told him never to go to Australia. He asked why. I replied with the following: "If you're walking down the street and some Australian recognizes you, the first words out of his mouth will be 'G'day, Gadau'!"

Ice Cream Pizza

Kathy, Misch, and I were working baggage. Our next arrival was in three hours. Misch suggested we order out pizza. I wanted ice cream. Kathy said, "Rosa's Pizza has Ben and Jerry's ice cream on their menu. Why don't we order ice cream and have it delivered?"

It was a brilliant idea. I called Rosa's Pizza. I ordered three pints of ice cream from their menu.

The guy on the other end of the phone line asked, "You don't want any pizza?"

I told him we did not; we just wanted the ice cream, and we wanted Rosas to deliver it. They did. We paid and added a big tip. We pigged out. Yum.

Pictures in Baggage Service

I asked my station manager if I could put some pictures on the walls of the baggage service office.

He asked, "What kind?"

I replied, "Bilbo Baggins and Darth Vader!"

"Why those?" he said.

"Because Bilbo Baggins lived in 'Bag End,' and Darth Vader because anyone who enters the baggage service office knows they are going to the Dark Side!" His answer was a vehement "no!"

Baggage Service Quotes

Another time, I asked my station manager if I could place quotes over the top of the baggage service office door and behind our counter on the back wall.

He asked, "What kind of quotes?"

I replied, "'Abandon all hope ye who enter here' from Dante's Inferno over the front door, and 'Against stupidity the gods themselves contend in vain!' from Plato on the back wall."

He said, "Why those?"

I responded, "The quote by Dante because people know their luggage is missing when they enter the office, and the quote from Plato because even Plato knew you can't change stupid people!"

Again, he said, "No!"

Voice Mail

I called a student to tell him his suitcase had arrived. Here is the voice mail I heard: "Hey, this is Joel. If I don't answer, I'm out partying, and if this is Horizon Airlines, you'd better damn well have my suitcase!"

Password

Cortney and I were again working together. The "private" telephone rang into the baggage office.

I answered. "May I speak with Cortney?"

"What's the password?" I asked.

"Father" was the reply!

"That'll work!"

Family Dog

A certain family here in Spokane used to have a car business in Billings, Montana. They would fly all the time between the two cities. Whenever they did fly, however, they would always try to fly on a bereavement fare, a reduced fare given for a death in the family.

One day this family member checked in at the ticket counter with Toni. The girl said she was flying on a bereavement fare to Billings. Everyone knew this family tried to scam everyone and everything all the time.

Toni asked her one question: "Who died this time...the family dog?"

AIR FORCE

Do you know what was so nice about being an Air Force Navigator? By an act of Congress, I could legally tell pilots where to go!

When I was in Sacramento for initial navigator training, the Officers' Club still had gambling, smoking, and a "stag bar." Women weren't allowed to fly at that time. The entire family housing units consisted of male bachelors! It was TGIF (Thank God I Fly), and the "stag bar" was very crowded. This was 1971 so we still had lots of sixties attitudes: Ban the bra; Turn on, Tune in, Drop Out; If It Feels Good, Do It; and Make Love, Not War!

The barmaid had dark red hair, was physically well endowed, and never wore a bra. One day a student had been drinking since noon. He was so "toasted" that he had to rest his chin on his hands on top of the bar. The barmaid was standing in front of him with her arms folded across her tummy. The student looked up in his bleary haze, saw what was in front of him, and asked: "Are those real?" The barmaid lifted up her sweater and replied, "They sure as hell are!" The guy fell off his bar stool, passed out, and we had to carry him to his room. After the barmaid finished her shift that day, she didn't have to buy a drink for the rest of the night!

As my crew was planning for our combat mission to Vietnam, a lieutenant colonel approached our table and said, "Captain Stuter, follow me—and bring your gear." I threw my mission planning items into my navigator's bag, followed the LC to a truck, and he drove us out toward the airfield. A navigator had gotten sick just as his plane was to takeoff. I was his replacement. A B-52 was sitting at the "hammerhead" waiting for me.

I took my gear, threw it into the plane, climbed up the hatch, and began to close it. The pilot had already begun his roll across the "hold line." I got the door latched and buckled into my seat just as the plane lifted off the ground. For twelve hours I flew a combat mission without knowing any crew names, the crew number, or where they were originally stationed. All I knew was that the radar-navigator's name was Al who was seated to my left!

Here at Fairchild AFB, Roy was our Operations Officer. He was a real pain in the ass. He kept interrupting our mission planning, briefings, and crew study daily. Most of the time, the crews paid no attention to him. How could he get the crews' attention? He bought a whistle! He would walk into the Ops area, blow the whistle, and say what he wanted to say. This got very annoying, even to the enlisted administrative personnel. One day Roy was in a hurry to make a big announcement to everyone. He ran into his office, grabbed the whistle—and almost pulled his arm out of its socket. The enlisted admin people had glued the damned whistle to his desk! Even they hated it! Roy never blew that whistle again.

I flew 27 combat missions between Guam and Southeast Asia (Vietnam, Laos, and Cambodia). The only land mass between Guam and SEA was the Philippine Islands. All else was ocean. After the war ended, our Wing, both bombers and tankers, returned to Fairchild. That's when the Air Force in all its infinite wisdom decided to send me to Water Survival training!

Did you know that military intelligence is an oxymoron!

We used to pull satellite alert out of Fairchild at Glasgow, Montana. The base had been closed years before we got there, but we pulled alert there to help keep the Russians at bay during the Cold War. Roy was on alert with us. Every few days the bombers had to be moved forward or aft of their parking positions. They were fully fueled, and if a bomber sat in one place too long, the wheels would flatten under all that weight. Roy asked to be pushed backward from his parked spot. The tug driver pushed too far, and the aft trucks of the plane sank into the unreinforced concrete pad behind it. Roy had to start all eight engines, and apply a lot of power to get the aft trucks out and back into proper parking position. Ever after, that sunken pad of concrete was nicknamed "Roy's ruts!"

One day our mission was to fly almost to the North Pole from Fairchild. We were to practice polar navigation procedures, as well as simulate an attack from Russia on the United States. Since this was peacetime, we had to make position reports the entire way northbound and to a certain point southbound before we began our low-level bombing simulation. We called this one post on the DEW (Distant Early Warning) Line somewhere up in northern Canada. The copilot called in the report. The guy on the ground asked about the World Series. The copilot told him about it. The guy asked another question. After almost fifteen minutes of an Air Force version of "Twenty Questions," the copilot asked, "Why are you asking us all these questions?"

The guy on the ground radioed back and said, "Because you're the first people I've talked to in a week!"

We had a Dining in at Fairchild. This was a formal dinner amongst our squadron's officer personnel which usually consisted of a high-ranking officer as a guest speaker. This day we had a two-star general to speak. In the middle of the speech, a guy rushed into the room holding up a box and yelled, "Pizza man for General Smith!" The General was stunned; he had certainly not ordered a pizza. No. All the Second Lieutenants in the squadron had ordered the pizza, and they had paid this guy to deliver it in the middle of the General's speech! The general was embarrassed, and the pizza delivery man went home rich. It was awesome!

The Wing Commander decided that once per month a formal flag-lowering retreat would be held. A B-52 was also to pass over as the flag was lowered. Well, it was a great idea, but a disaster in practice! The pilots in the squadron began to take bets on which of them could fly the lowest and the fastest over the flagpole. My friend, Jim, won the bet. As the last pilot to ever perform this ritual, he flew so low and so fast that half the windows in the nearby headquarters building were blown out!

One day our crew was getting ready to fly out of Fairchild. We arrived at the plane, and the pilot began to brief us on the previous maintenance write-ups. Many times Captain Smith would write CND (Can Not Duplicate), FAI (Fly As Is) to clear the aircraft to fly. That day the pilot refused to fly the plane because he felt the problem was too dangerous to be released. The pilot asked the crew chief to call in to Maintenance Control and get Capt.

Smith out to the plane to personally tell us why he signed off this potentially dangerous condition.

After fifteen minutes, the crew chief returned to our bus. "Is Capt. Smith on his way here?" asked the pilot.

"No, sir," replied the sergeant.

"Why not? I want Capt. Smith to explain why he signed-off this write-up. Get him here immediately!"

"I can't, sir," said the sergeant.

"And why?"

"Captain Smith permanently departed the base six months ago!"

The Maintenance Division had been "pencil-whipping" the maintenance problems so that the planes would fly, and the Wing Commander's monthly statistics looked good!

Remember: Safety first. Yeah, right!

A B-52 was flying north when the navigator called over the radio: "Pilot, turn right ninety degrees and hold that heading for three minutes." The pilot turned the aircraft.

Three minutes later, the navigator called the pilot and told him to turn left ninety degrees and hold that heading for three minutes. The pilot turned again. Next, the navigator stated to turn left ninety degrees and hold that heading for three minutes. The aircraft was turned.

At last the navigator called the pilot to turn right ninety degrees and continue on course.

"Nav, what the hell did we just do?" an irritated pilot asked.

The navigator retorted with, "I was eating my flight lunch, and I dropped mustard on my chart, so we navigated around it!"

My base commander at Zaragoza AB, Spain, had a barbecue for all the officers under his command. It was a totally casual affair. I wore a tee shirt with "Do it in the BUFF" on the front with a front-view of a B-52 underneath. BUFF (Big Ugly Fat Fellow) is the unofficial nickname for a B-52, among others!

As I approached the Colonel's wife to chat, she looked at the tee shirt and stated, "Do it in the BUFF. Wayne and I have been doing it in the buff ever since we were married!" Enough said.

At U-Tapao AB, Thailand, my copilot, Rich, and I were housed in a twenty-foot trailer. It consisted of five feet on each end as bedroom and reading space. The middle was ten feet of shower, toilet, and two sinks. One morning we were each shaving. We each wore only a sarong. The Thai maid came in to clean the area where we were. She saw us only covered by sarongs, put her hand over her face in surprise, and said in broken English, "Me no lookee I Me no lookee!" all the while peeking through her spread open fingers at us.

Rich looked at me, and I looked at him. At the same moment, Rich said, "Let's do it!"

We each grabbed an arm of the maid, and all three of us ended in the shower, she fully-clothed! All she did was laugh!

Our crew walked to the Officers' Club to eat one day in U-Tapao. The waitress came by with the menus, all the while wearing a very short skirt and a skimpy blouse. Someone ordered a hamburger.

The waitress replied, "No hab hamburger. Hab cheeseburger!"

"But I want a hamburger," the crewmember said.

"No hab hamburger. Hab cheeseburger."

"Then make me a cheeseburger, and before you cook it, take off the cheese."

"No can do, GI! Only hab cheeseburger!"

Another time, we were in the bar at U-Tapao. The copilot was a tea-totaler. The waitress, as usual, wore a very short skirt topped with a very low-cut, skimpy blouse. The outfit looked more like a bikini than anything else. Everyone ordered their drinks except the copilot, who ordered iced tea.

As she passed out our drinks after a few rounds, the pilot asked the copilot, "Wouldn't you just like to grab some of that?"

"No," the copilot answered, "God wouldn't let me do that!"

After another round, the pilot asked the copilot, "Would you like to drink some orange juice instead of tea?"

The copilot replied, "Yes."

The pilot walked up to the bar and ordered a double-shot screwdriver. He brought it back to the table and gave it to the copilot.

We were getting a little rowdy, and the conversation got a lot more animated. The copilot heartily joined in, quickly downing his drink. With the glass empty, he asked the pilot to get him another orange juice. Again, the pilot ordered a double-shot screwdriver! He returned to the table, and he gave the copilot the drink.

About halfway through the drink, the bar maid came by for another order. She bent over right in front of the copilot to clean up all the "dead soldiers," (empty glasses). The copilot looked at what was hanging in front of him, turned to the pilot, and announced, "Wouldn't you just like to bite into that?"

The pilot smugly replied, "No, God wouldn't let me do that!"

"We are the unwilling, led by the unknowing, are doing the impossible for the ungrateful. We have done so much with so little for so long we are now qualified to do everything with nothing."

Our crew was passing through Hickam AFB, Honolulu, Hawaii. Rich and I were passing through the MAC (Military Airlift Command) terminal. There were many Marines sitting around waiting to fly to the States.

Rich said in a loud voice, "What are all these Jarheads doing sitting here?"

I said to Rich, "We're dead!" as six Marines stood up and began to walk toward us.

In a booming voice behind us, we heard, "What are all the Jarheads doing here?" All the Marines turned around and sat back down. We turned around only to see an Army Colonel behind us. I could have bought him drinks all day to thank him!

At Minot AFB, North Dakota, the Headquarters building had the word "PRIDE" painted on the side of the building in huge letters. It was supposed to mean "Personal Responsibility in Daily Endeavors." The non-pilot crewmembers told me that it actually meant "Pilots Regenerate Ignorance Despite Education!"

Also at Minot, above the front gate to the base reads a sign which says: "Only the Best Go North." Unfortunately, whoever designed the sign forgot to complete the sentence: "But Only the Smart Stay South!"

One day I went to use the latrine while on Alert duty at Minot. When I finished, I noticed an M-16 rifle standing in a corner. I grabbed the rifle and took it to the CO's (Charge of Quarters) desk. The sergeant about crapped his pants when he saw what I hand in my hand.

"Where did you find that?" he asked.

"In the latrine," I replied.

The CQ made an all-facility announcement, and a few minutes later a Second Lieutenant appeared from around the corner. He knew that he was in deep s***!

"It's mine," he stated. The CQ gave him the weapon, and I took the frightened lieutenant away from the desk for a private conversation.

"You realize I can turn you in to your squadron commander for this, don't you?"

"Yes, sir," he replied.

"I'm not going to do so, though. However, you will not get away with this Scott-free. Thursday morning after Alert changeover about 1000, you had better be standing outside the Alert facility gate with a case of Coors beer in your arms!"

"I will, sir. I will," he replied in a frightened voice.

When Thursday morning arrived, we got off Alert duty and headed to our cars. There was the lieutenant right outside the Alert gate with the case of Coors in his arms, just as required! Those cans of beer tasted awfully good!

My crew had to fly a B-52 down to Bergstrom AFB in Austin, Texas, for a static display for an ROTC class. The aircraft tour took about an hour. We had the rest of the day free, so we went bar hopping.

In the first bar, the copilot said proudly, "I'll buy the first round." We, five of us, all ordered double shots! He was not happy. In the second bar, the copilot ordered a Singapore Sling.

The bartender said, "I can't make that for you."

"Why?" the copilot asked.

The bartender responded, "This is Texas. We don't make them sissy drinks in this bar!" The copilot never got served either.

Another time my Air Force friend Bob and I were bar hopping in Fort Worth, Texas. We met a sweet, young girl, and Bob was trying to make time with her. She finally asked, "Where are y'all from?"

I replied, "Pennsylvania."

She said, "Uh, a Yankee!" "Bob, where are you all from?"

Bob said, "New Hampshire."

She responded, "Uh, a damned Yankee!"

We had just ferried a bomber to Andersen AFB, Guam. Henry was a black instructor-navigator. The base had no sleeping accommodations for us, so we had to be bussed in a Blue Goose downtown to a hotel on the beach. Shucks!

As we left the Main Gate, our female driver asked, "Are you guys thirsty?" Of course we were! From behind her seat, she pulled out a gallon of wine. "Here you go!" We began to pass the jug around amongst us.

Henry was sitting in the seat right behind the driver. After ten minutes the airman said, "Sir, may I ask you a question?"

Henry replied, "Yes."

"Is it true that all black men have rhythm?"

Henry replied, "I don't know about the rhythm part, but all them other stories are true!"

A girl named Diane lived upstairs from me in the Bachelor Officers Quarters (BOO) on Guam. I kept asking her out on dates, but she kept saying no. One day during a cookout, I asked, "Diane, I keep asking you out, and you keep saying no. Why?"

She responded with, "You only have two of the three qualities I look for in dates. You're an officer, and you are on flying status."

"What am I missing?"

Diane stated, "You're not married." I never spoke to her again.

The showers in the BOQs (Bachelor Officers Quarters) on Guam had open tops, and the water pipes could be seen going up to the next floor. I sang a lot every time I took a shower! One day the girl who lived upstairs from me told me that I sang really well. I told her that she must be tone deaf. "As a matter of fact I am," she replied!

One time on Guam, B-52H units were deployed from the States as part of their Operational Readiness Inspections. The units would stay three months, fly home, and be replaced by other B-52H units. One unit had a lieutenant colonel who owned a hand puppet.

One time as I passed the colonel's door, I saw him reprimanding a pilot from their squadron. The colonel wasn't doing it; the puppet was! This captain was being "chewed out" by a hand puppet! Word through our squadron was that the puppet did all the dirty work, and the colonel got all the glory.

When the colonel was directly asked about some of his actions, he denied everything. He didn't do any of it; the puppet did. He was serious, too!

While I was on Guam, we used to fly twelve-hour practice missions over South Korea and Australia. We never landed there. Australia lies in the Southern Hemisphere. The first time we "crossed the line" (equator), I crawled up to the cockpit with a small cup of water and asked the pilot to pour some over my helmet. He did. I poured a little over his helmet, and he poured a little water over the copilot's helmet.

On my way downstairs to the navigators' stations, I stopped and poured water over the helmet of the electronic warfare officer. I also poured the last bit of water from the cup over the navigator's helmet before returning to my seat. I called on the radio to the gunner (who was sitting in the tail) to pour a little water over his helmet.

After we had all done that, the copilot cried, "Why the hell did the navigator pour water over us?"

"Well," I said, "the U.S. Navy has an initiation ceremony for new sailors who have never crossed the equator before. It's a little difficult to throw you overboard from 36,000 feet!"

We used to practice sea surveillance missions from Guam. These missions consisted of two B-52s flying a search pattern with the latest intelligence information to locate unknown ships. Our "targets" were normally the U.S. Navy.

One day we were to look for a three-ship column of cruisers and destroyers. After some intense searching, we located the ships, and completed our assigned tasks for the day. We were to make one more pass. The captain of this little group told us to "make it a good one." We flew out about ten miles and got behind the ships. They were in a triangle formation.

As we approached, each "BUFF" aligned beside the other so the planes would fly through the inner spaces between the ships. As the planes reached the sterns of the rear ships, each began a forty-five-degree climb. Each plane's Electronic Warfare Officers then dumped bundles of chaff all over the ships. Those sailors probably swept the decks for a week picking up all that aluminum foil. We made it "a good one!"

On another sea surveillance mission, we looked for seven U.S. Navy ships. We located them, accomplished the required maneuvers, and were ready to go home. The captain of the group asked our aircraft commander for one last pass because he had dignitaries onboard. We complied. We descended to about 100 feet above the water. Because we were so low and used an aircraft with eight screaming engines, the pass produced large "rooster tails" of water behind us.

We climbed, rejoined with the second aircraft, and returned to Guam. A week later, our aircraft commander was hauled in to the Wing Commander's office and severely reprimanded for the mission. It seems one of the dignitaries had a camera and took pictures of the "rooster tail" pass!

My friend, Norm, was the Wing Weather Officer on Guam. One time the island had two different typhoons approaching—one from the southwest and one from the southeast. When typhoons approached, the wing commander had to decide when to typhoon evacuate the B-52s to Okinawa. In the 80s, the National Weather Service was just beginning to give female names to typhoons; before that, all typhoons were named as males. The typhoons this time were named with a boy's name and a girl's name.

Norm was giving his weather briefing when the wing commander asked, "What would happen if these two typhoons merge as one big one?"

Norm replied, "Sir, we're going to have phoonication!"

The Wing Weather Office on Guam had a "weather rock." It was a tripod of sticks with a white rock suspended in the middle. A piece of paper was taped to the base of this tepee. It read: "If the rock is bright, it's sunny. If the rock is wet, it's raining. If the rock is moving, it's windy; and if the rock is missing, it's stolen!"

My navigator and his wife had just had a new baby girl. Three months later, our entire crew, baby and all, went to the Officers' Club for dinner. Well into the meal, the baby began to cry. The mother could not stop this. Everything she tried did not work. Everyone was getting irritated.

Finally, I said to Mike, my navigator, "I know what the baby needs."

"How do you know?" he replied.

"You're single!"

"Mike, I know what the baby needs," I said again.

"Alright," he said. "Go for it."

With that, I got up, walked over to the crib, picked up the tiny girl, placed her gently on my shoulder, and left. I walked the baby for ten minutes around the club. When I returned, the little girl was sound asleep. I gently placed her back into the crib, sat down, and continued to eating.

"How did you do that?" Mike asked.

"Easy," I replied. "Every girl knows her real father!!"

I got off Alert duty and drove to a friend's house to pick up some items. Pat had also been on Alert with me, too. I drove to the house, parked, and knocked on the door. Sylvia, Pat's wife, opened the door wearing only a robe and yelled, "Hi, honey!" as she flashed her robe open!

"Whoops, you're not honey!" she said, realizing that I was not her husband.

I asked Sylvia for the item, and she demurely found it and handed it to me. I returned to the car, and as I was driving away, here comes Pat driving home. I wonder if he got the same reception?

Before 1990 Strategic Air Command (SAC), Military Airlift Command (MAC), and Tactical Air Command (TAC) were three of the major flying divisions. The crewmembers said that the only good SAC was a paper sack; the only good MAC was a Big Mac; and the only good TAC was a thumb tack!

MISCELLANEOUS

How can you tell you have a pilot at your party? He'll tell you!

Why do you call a pilot a pilot? Because he piles it here, and piles it there, and piles it everywhere he goes!

How can you get a pilot not to talk? Have him sit on his hands! (When a pilot tells his flying stories, he always uses his hands to demonstrate).

You can always tell a pilot, but you can never tell him much!

Why did the flight attendant get pregnant? Pilot error!

Flight attendants used to be called stewardesses. Their motto: "Coffee, tea, or me." Whatever happened to the "me" part?

How can you tell you have a flight attendant at your party? She's the one sitting in the rear of the room with her plate on her knees wiping her fingers on the curtains, and every time a bell rings, she looks up!

One of the best airline cartoons that I ever saw had the jet bridge pulled away from the aircraft. The main cabin door was closed, and a man was splayed spread-eagled across the closed door. The caption underneath read: "When better late than never doesn't apply!"

We have dachshunds for dogs. One day they proved why dogs are a man's best friend and not a woman's. A squirrel was in the front yard. I opened the screen door, and three dogs ran toward the squirrel. The squirrel ran toward the tree. The dogs chased the squirrel. The squirrel ran around the bottom of the tree and along the fence. There were three male dachshunds barking up this tree! The squirrel was long gone. I looked at them and thought, "Typical guys! They learn it one way and never change. If they had been females, they would have looked around and asked for directions!"

A squirrel was out in the backyard. I opened the door, and Scooter ran toward the squirrel. The squirrel ran toward the fence. Scooter chased the squirrel. The first squirrel was playing with a second squirrel. The second squirrel ran down his tree and began chasing Scooter. It's squirrel-dachshund-squirrel running in a line across the backyard! The first squirrel ran through the fence.

Scooter hit the fence and began jumping up and down and barking. The second squirrel passed Scooter and ran through the fence as well. Scooter did a double-take and almost had a heart attack because he never knew that he was being chased by a squirrel!

One night as I arrived home from work, I saw that my wife had lined our driveway and sidewalk with blue yard lights.

My first thought was this: "Do I need to call in and ask permission to land?"

Why "Mother Nature" and "Father Time" are called so: "Mother Nature" has a woman's nickname because a woman's feelings and attitudes are as changeable as the weather; "Father Time," on the other hand, has a man's nickname because he is slow and methodical year in and year out, and everyone knows exactly what he is going to do!

When we were in Minot, our house was located a half mile from the local Dairy Queen. One day my wife and younger daughter put on their snow pants, winter boots, woolly mittens, and furry caps and walked to DQ. The day was ten degrees below zero with a foot of snow.

When the girls reached the store, my wife ordered two Peanut Buster parfaits. The woman behind the counter cried, "Do you know how cold it is outside?"

"Yes," my wife answered, "but we still want two Peanut Buster parfaits, please."

"Why?" asked the woman.

My wife smiled and said, "Because our chocolate low-level lights are blinking!"

The day was bright, sunny, and warm. My wife put on a spring-like dress. She looked great! As she walked around our Jeep Cherokee to get inside, a German stopped his car right beside her to gawk. My wife is probably the only woman in the world who was able to stop a speeding German with one pair of legs!

We had just visited Mount Rushmore in South Dakota. It had rained all day, and the weather was very gloomy. We toured the Visitors' Center and took the obligatory photographs. As I drove down the mountain, all of a sudden the clouds broke around us, and everything was bathed in bright sunshine! A beautiful end of the rainbow suddenly appeared directly in front of the car. "Look girls! It's the end of the rainbow," I exclaimed. "We're rich!"

"Dad," my younger daughter said in a droll voice, "the pot of gold is at the other end!"

A woman walked down a street in a little town in Germany. She passed a parking lot where a German man was changing clothes. He was completely naked. Yes, they do that.

"Ooh gross!" the woman screamed.

The German returned a broad smile and replied, "Danke schoen."

Gross in German means big!

A girl named Alicia owed me a dozen homemade chocolate chip cookies for working for her. She lived about five miles from the airport.

"When will I get my cookies?" I asked.

"Tomorrow," she replied.

Tomorrow arrived, and I asked Alicia, "Did you bring my chocolate chip cookies today?"

She reluctantly gave me an empty paper bag! "Where are the cookies?" I exclaimed.

"They were in the bag when I left the house!"

Alicia had eaten a dozen homemade chocolate chip cookies in five miles!

What do men want most in life? The answer is the letter S: Sex, Suds, Sports, Speed, Status, Steak, and Sons!

It's time to close this session of Byrdman's Travels. Next time, you will have to tell the stories. My last thought is this: "True friends never part when remembrance is in the heart." Take care.

What Is Enough?

I went temporary duty to U-Tapao AB, Thailand, in 1975. At the time, all of Vietnam was collapsing under the onslaught of the Viet Cong. The Viet Cong began to steamroll from the Demilitarized Zone (DMZ) down the coast and the inland cities toward Saigon.

The Vietnam War had ended 15 January 1973. We flew combat missions to Laos and Cambodia until 15 August 1973. After that time, all combat troops were removed from "in-country." We still had a military presence on Guam, Thailand, the Philippines, Okinawa, and Taipei.

I met a girl at U-Tapao, and I lived with her half of my five-month tour. We ate sticky rice, lily pads, and baked bananas with real honey comb inside. The house was one-room. The toilet area consisted of a concrete slab with a hole in the middle. A large cask of water containing a ladle stood next to the concrete. We shopped at the local market. The aromas were interesting. Everything from fruits and vegetables to dripping naked chickens hanging from a clothesline were before us. The heat and the high humidity added to the "flavor" of the open market. I learned to trade and barter there. You make a price; I respond. You disagree. You make a lower price. We banter back-and-forth until a common price is agreeable to both parties.

It was simple living: flying during the day, eating and drinking in the evening, and making love at night.

Then I returned back to Spokane. I was sent on another temporary duty to Carswell AFB in Fort Worth, Texas. On a day off, I walked into my first Wal-Mart store. I almost vomited. All I saw were aisles upon aisles of stuff piled three tiers high. I was physically ill. What was this? Where did all this come from? Why did anyone need any of this?

What is enough: Wal-Mart or a one-room house in Thailand?

The Light Bulb

I was talking with my Spanish neighbors. We were discussing youth and getting older. My Spanish was sloppy at best and atrocious at worst. I was trying to illustrate how people changed physically as they aged. I spied a light bulb sitting on the kitchen counter. I picked up the light bulb by the small end and held it upright.

In Spanish, I said "joven" (young). I turned the light bulb upside down and stated "viejo" (old). In one easy movement, I went from young to old!

Friendship versus Religion

Ray and I had been friends forever. He owned a music store in my hometown, as well as a Christian bookstore in an adjacent town. We were both Protestants. He was Mennonite; I was not.

Ray would often invite me to worship with him whenever I was home on military leave. Even though Vietnam was raging in the news every day, I enjoyed the Mennonite worship for its simplicity, straight forward message, and friendly people. I was always accepted by them.

One leave Ray invited me to services as always. I stated that we might have a problem. "Why?" he asked.

I said, "If I go to church with you, my father will have to drive me to Harrisburg after the services so I can fly back to Spokane. I must be in my military uniform to fly. Won't I 'stick out like a sore thumb' in my uniform, especially in a Mennonite church?"

"Come to worship anyway," Ray replied.

So I did. There I sat in my dress Air Force uniform in the midst of a congregation filled with pacifists and conscientious objectors!

After the service, Ray and I walked out and shook the pastor's hand at the doorway. I immediately found my father's car, and we speedily went to Harrisburg.

Ten years' later, I was again home on leave. Ray and I met together at a local restaurant for lunch.

As we chatted, Ray said, "Remember that Sunday when you wore your uniform to church?"

"How could I ever forget?" I replied.

"Well, the church Elders 'called me on the carpet' for that. They wanted to excommunicate me from the church!"

"I told you that we'd have problems with that! So what happened next?" I asked.

"Well," Ray continued, "they asked me why I brought a military man into their church in full uniform. I told them that I did it out of friendship. The Elders were astonished! They asked me how a man who proclaimed to be a pacifist could bring a military man to our church out of friendship, even though you'd been there many times before in civilian clothes. I told the Elders because of our friendship that I did it. The Elders were flabbergasted! I then posed a question to them: I asked them which was more important, a friend worshipping in my church under my beliefs or the uniform he wore. The uniform, I added, which represented the country in which we live and which was established to protect against religious persecution; a country in which we practice religious freedom today."

"So, what did the Elders say to that?" I asked, fully intrigued.

"What could they say?" Ray responded. "They allowed me to remain with the church!"

We both celebrated the victory by enjoying ice cream for dessert. Together—as friends.

"Spasiba"

During my military career, I spent thirteen of my twenty years overseas. I lived in Spain, Germany, Guam, and Minot, North Dakota. Minot isn't overseas, but if you've ever lived there, civilization, namely Fargo and Minneapolis, seem very far away and very foreign!

I was working in the baggage office for Horizon Air one evening. A couple had just flown in from Moscow, Russia, and their luggage did not accompany them. It was delayed in Customs at John F. Kennedy Airport in New York City and would not arrive until the following day.

The couple spoke no English. Their daughter, a student at Gonzaga University, did all the translating. I asked the usual questions: What style are the bags; what color; what are specific contents; and what is a local address and telephone number needed for delivery after the luggage arrived? The daughter provided all the information.

After my report was completed, I handed the daughter our receipt for the lost luggage. It contained the record locator for the claim, as well as our telephone number. The family began to leave the office when I spoke the word "spasiba." That means "thank you" in Russian.

Upon hearing something spoken to them in their native language, both parents gave me the hugest smiles I ever saw! This was the answer to my daily prayer of trying to do something kind for someone.

MAKING AMENDS

My first experience was when my brother, Gary, decided to move to Spokane in 1975. I was going temporary duty to U-Tapao AB, Thailand, from January to May. Since he would be here during my absence, I agreed to let him "apartment sit" while I was away. The apartment was two-bedroom with all the amenities. After I returned, I basically kicked him out and told him to find a place of his own. I really didn't want him around me. I was too busy "doing my own thing."

A second experience happened in 1977. I was between assignments from Fairchild AFB to Andersen AFB, Guam. I went home to my hometown in Pennsylvania on leave for three weeks. My sister and her family were visiting, as well. I don't remember the details. I just remember that I got into an argument with someone, probably my father, and I left the house irate. My nephew, Jason, who was about six years old, came out of the house to wave good-bye. I saw him wave as I drove off, and I certainly didn't wave back.

The last experience happened in 1990 after I had retired from the Air Force. My family and I were in transition between Germany and Spokane. We spent a week at my parents' house before travelling west. I don't remember these details either. I only remember that my wife and my father got into a heated argument. I just remember that my wife decided to pack up and leave for Spokane after it. No discussion. We did so; my wife hated my parents ever after. She never wanted to call them, talk to them, or even hear about them anymore in her life.

When my father died in 2010 and I wasn't able to get home for the funeral (weather, Christmas rush, and no seats), my wife never mentioned anything about my family during that time. I never even got a hug for condolences!

After these three experiences and many others, I became a whole lot older and a whole lot wiser, I knew I had to make amends.

Fast forward to June 2013. Last year when I went back to Pennsylvania for my mother's ninetieth birthday, I stayed with Gary and his wife, and my sister stayed in a cottage at Valley View Rest Home. It was the first time since 1969 that the three children were again together at home at the same time. Anyway, Gary drove me to State College so I could fly to Spokane at the end of the week. During the ride, I apologized to him for "throwing him to the wolves," so to speak, in 1975. I should have left him stay with me in the other bedroom. Then he could have found his own footing in life, not have hardly any living expenses, and possibly found a better job other than a cook.

This year when I returned for my mother's funeral, I was in the middle of a divorce, my finances were a mess, and my future was pretty bleak. My sister, her husband, and Jason were there, as well.

Sometime during the week, Jason and I had a heart-to-heart talk about my leaving in a rage in 1977. He broached the subject first. It had bothered him all these years as much as it had bothered me. I had a guilty conscience. We discussed it, I truly apologized for my actions, and we came to a satisfying understanding between us. Nothing was ever mentioned from my wife or older daughter about either parent's death to me. My younger daughter did stay in touch as best she could from Arkansas.

What all this comes down to is this: I returned to Pennsylvania for a birthday party and a funeral in two consecutive years for my mother. One was a high point, and the other was a low point. Both times the focus was on my mother, but I firmly believe that God used these times for me to make amends with my family and my sister's family. He used these occasions for me to atone for the errors of my past. He also used these occasions to make me a better person who valued family over self.

THE BEACH

I was lying on the living room floor one afternoon watching television. I was barefoot and dressed in a white t-shirt and a pair of scraggly cutoff blue jeans made into a pair of shorts.

My younger daughter breezed through on her way out to sit on the front porch swing. She stopped, took one look at me, and said, "Dad, you look like a beached whale!"

Then she sped quickly out the front door. I groaned. She had just ruined any chance of my going to the beach on vacation ever again. I could envision it now: Me lying on my beach blanket face up in the sand; the sound of the surf rumbling onto the shoreline, crashing against the smooth sand in front of me. Unfortunately, I couldn't very well see the surf or those waves. All I could see from my supine position were all these Greenpeace participants walking around my towel carrying handmade cardboard placards. Hey, didn't they know they were blocking my view of the sun, as well as the ocean? Around in a circle this group walked. I slowly rolled onto my stomach to hide the sunburn I'd received. As I did so, I glanced at one of the placards which each person carried. I groaned in agony. To my dismay, the placard read the following: "Save the Whale!" I pulled the corner of my beach blanket over my head to shut out the protest march.

Corky

The first time we met we were instant friends. She was young, brunette, average height, lithe, very Mormon, very married, and very pregnant. She was beautiful! I was thirty years her senior, old, gray, fat, and married, too. She had transferred from Anchorage where she worked for Alaska Airlines to Spokane to work for Horizon Air. Her husband built web sites for a living, and they already had two children. Corky was thirty years old.

We worked evenings together in the baggage office. She and her family travelled a lot back and forth to Anchorage or to Utah. Whenever she returned, she always had a huge smile to greet me, and I always updated her on the news of the airline or of Spokane station. We worked well together. She was devoted to her faith, family, and friends. She had high morals and strong family values. Me? I was a flirt, a jokester, a retired officer, a troubled married man, and a senior airline employee.

Because Corky travelled so much, she would always need extra days off. Whenever I could, I would always work for her on those days. Sometimes it meant my working twelve days straight, but I cared not. As long as she could get to where she wanted to go, I was more than willing to help her.

Why did I do this? Maybe it was an old man's delusions of grandeur of making a younger woman happy. It was definitely out of friendship. Could it be more than that? Never! She was deeply loved by her husband, and she deeply loved him, as well. Maybe I did it as an escape mechanism from a failing marriage. I don't really know. I do know that she was deeply grateful for my working or helping her. She always repaid me with dozens of homemade chocolate chip cookies!

We discussed everything. Nothing was forbidden. She didn't divulge much about personal family problems as I did, but she did discuss her travels, her children, and her lack of being buxom.

As my life began to totally unravel, she wished only that I do what was required to "have a right to be happy." She had three more children in the time she worked with me. Later in our friendship, she would always greet me with a hug no matter if we were alone, in public, or if her husband were present. We shared dinners at her home with the entire family present, and she even invited me to see one of her sons being baptized. Not in the church temple, of course. Her friends accepted me and greatly praised me for working so many nights and weekends for her so all of them could travel together. She no longer works for Horizon Air. We still keep in touch. She and her family will be moving shortly to Florida; I may never see her again. I do know that we care for each other. Her leaving will affect me greatly. l will be losing, in a sense, a true and very dear friend. She said it would be bittersweet for her too. We do have one thing that will always keep us together however: "True friends never part when remembrance is in the heart."

A Fork in the Road

One of Yogi Berra's famous quotes states the following: "When you come to a fork in the road, take it!" Here is an example of that.

BOY: "You know what I'd like to do right now?"

GIRL: "Sleep with me!"

BOY: "Besides that. I'd like for us to take the dogs for a long walk. You know what else I'd like to do?"

GIRL: "Have sex with me!"

BOY: "Besides that. After walking the dogs, we should all go for ice cream. You know what else we should do after that?"

GIRL: "Make love to me!"

BOY: "You know, we are walking down two different roads of conversation, and my road is quickly merging into yours. Soon we will come to a fork in the road. I'll take it!"

My First Deer Hunt

The time is November 1959 in Pennsylvania. Thanksgiving is over. The upcoming Monday is an undeclared state holiday throughout the state. It is the first day of buck season. I am twelve years old. My father, grandfather, and I drive into the mountains that Sunday afternoon to set up camp. We are to use an old, unused cabin of a friend. The weather is crisp. There is no snow. We park the pickup truck. The dead fallen leaves crunch under our boots as we make our way to the cabin. Bright sunshine blazes through the myriad of maple, oak, ash, walnut, and white pine trees. The cabin isn't very far from where we parked. We easily find our way to it. My father unlocks the door.

We are here. Finally! We thud in to a cold, musty, unkempt one-room building with a heavily used fireplace. The three cots inside are covered in a light layer of dust. We brush off the dust, and the three of us lay out our sleeping bags atop each one. We open a cupboard. The mice run everywhere! Three mice made a nest in one corner of the cupboard. We chased two of them out the open front door. The third mouse hides in a corner. Stomp goes my Dad's boot! He picks up the dead mouse by its tail and throws it outside. That ends mouse patrol.

We set the food we brought inside the cupboard. We don't mind the dirt. We have only one thing in mind: Deer! After our victuals are stashed away, all three of us go outside to gather firewood. It is easy to find. There are no logging operations in this part of the state. We find lots of "squaw wood," dead wood easy to reach on lower branches. We use it for kindling. We find plenty of partly-rotted larger logs to build a good fire for the night.

The sun is quickly setting. With a good supply of wood inside the cabin—we put the wood inside to keep it dry in case snow falls overnight. We relax, light the old kerosene lantern my grandfather had brought, and make a good fire in the fireplace. We broke out our supper. We brought our own water because the cabin has no well. The meal consists of sandwiches and cold baked beans. We drink strong black coffee made in a pot that we set atop a corner of some embers in the fireplace.

Once our scant meal is finished, the three of us move the cots closer together. Each of us sits on his selected cot; we break out a deck of cards and play poker. We use no money; we play the game to while away the time before we crawl into our respective sleeping bags. Our conversation centers mostly on where each of us was going to hunt the next day, what each of us would do if he shot a deer, and how we would get it back to camp afterwards. Any bathroom chores are done behind the cabin. We use dried leaves for toilet paper. My father or grandfather, one of them, luckily remembers to bring a portable alarm clock.

It is bedtime. I crawl into my cold sleeping bag with all my clothes still on my body. I hadn't yet learned to take them off and place them in the bottom of the bag. I begin to sweat a lot. I listen to everything—even the pattering of more mice trying to get into the cupboard. My father and grandfather snore all night! I barely sleep. I definitely have a severe case of "buck fever!"

Ringgg! Ringgg! Clunk. "God damned alarm clock!" It is five A.M. We each crawl out from the warmth of our respective sleeping bags into a cold cabin. The fire in the fireplace is out. My grandfather makes a new fire as my father and I break out a breakfast of sausage sandwiches, more cold beans, and more strong coffee that is heated after the newly-made fire begins to roar.

The shivers we encounter from the cold cabin quickly turn to shivers of excitement for what the new day might bring. I dress in a woolen checkered shirt, blue jeans, and heavy brown work boots. My jacket, which my grandfather had given to me, consists of a brown, heavily grained, hunting coat. Its color blends exactly into all the brown leaves of the forest. For safety purposes, my father takes a very large red bandana and, using safety pins, pins it on the middle of the back of the coat. My official deer license is pinned over the bandana. I am using a 30-30 lever-action Winchester rifle. It is the perfect gun for hunting large game in central Pennsylvania. My father had won it on a punchboard at our local V.F.W., and he gave it to me as a gift. I still have it to this day. Buck season officially begins at eight o'clock in the morning. I stow a length of rope into the back of my coat to use to drag a deer back to camp.

About seven o'clock or so, after all the chores are done and we had brushed our teeth from a bucket of water using only toothpaste and our fingers, the three of us head out "into the wilderness," so to speak. It seems like wilderness to me. I grew up in the area, but everything around me awes me! I am very excited and very shaky. I am a true nimrod. If I did see a buck walk in front of me, can I even remember to put the rifle to my shoulder, aim, or even squeeze the trigger? If those actions actually happen, could I even hit the side of the mountain let alone a lone, free-standing buck? Only the future held those answers.

We three walk outside and load our rifles. We begin to walk to where we believe deer might be. The day is the same as the day prior had been: Bright, sunny, crisp, and very clear. My grandfather leaves us first. He and his wisdom know the perfect place to find deer and where to kill a buck. My father and I walk along the floor of the ridge. Dad is taking me to an old charcoal pit where charcoal had been made in the previous century. We arrive at the pit. Time and some erosion have levelled the pit to a small, leaf-covered, open flat of space. Dad places me in front of a tall oak tree. From there, I have a very large view of the entire uphill side of the mountain. Before Dad leaves me, he tells me if I do kill something to call and call and call until he gets to me. Off he goes to his own deer stand.

The morning is beautiful. Dried and dead leaves cover the ground. I can hear any movement for many yards. The trees are not so dense so my vision field sweeps over one hundred yards in every direction. I wait. The sun rises brightly in the sky. Early snow birds twitter and flutter amongst the remaining leaves on the trees. I hear nothing. I wait. Suddenly I hear a rustle in the leaves to my right. Whatever it is, it shuffles through the leaves, stops, shuffles again, and keeps moving toward me. The shuffling comes closer. There it is! Oh, it is only a gray squirrel. He is looking for his breakfast! Any old acorn will do. The squirrel continues his shuffling and haphazard journey through the leaves until he is finally out of my sight. I wait. I look everywhere. I listen. I look again. I see a slight movement to my left. It is above me. I look again. Deer! About thirty yards away. One, two, three! How many more are there? The group is slowly walking from my left to the center of my vision field.

Number one: Doe. Number two: Doe. Number three: Doe. Each slowly maneuvers her way along the ribbed little ridge above the charcoal pit. They walk. They stop. They listen. Each is very cautious. Each doe is as beautiful as the day: Brown coats, white underbellies, and the tell-tale flagging of their white tails at their ends. Wait! Another movement! Another deer! My heart begins to thump rapidly. I look. I gaze. All I can see are legs, body, and a brown coat. There is nothing more. Each time it pauses in its slow, cautious walk, its head is always obscured behind a tree or tree limb. My heart pounds even louder in my chest. Can the deer hear it? I wait with bated breath. Can it be? Is it? It moves. I look. Antlers! It is a buck! He trails the does, very cautious in his actions and very deliberate in his movements. My heart is pounding even louder. Its beats drown out every other sound! I am all eyes. With so many trees between us, I must wait for the buck to stop in an open space long enough for me to get a shot off. My bowels are in turmoil. I can pee in my pants, and it doesn't matter. I am that excited! The does stop. The buck keeps meandering forward. One doe steps out into an open space. I can see her head, neck, and shoulders clearly. It is my shot spot! I cock my hammer and slowly raise my rifle up to my shoulder. I wait. I try to breathe normally. It isn't happening. I try to even breathe. That is barely happening. My heart pounds like a Shawnee's drumbeat. Can the buck hear it? The lead doe moves ahead of the rest. The buck moves into her vacant position. He is open and in the clear! Tall, erect, and proud, his antlers glitter in the bright sunlight. I take aim. Time stops. Please, oh, please, don't move. I aim for the spot behind the shoulder blade. Squeeze the trigger slowly I tell myself. Breathe. I pull the trigger. BLAM! All the deer scatter. The does run everywhere, mainly uphill. The buck jolts to the left and vanishes. Had I hit it? Did I miss it? Breathe, Byrd, breathe. I walk up to the spot where I thought the buck last stood. My heart is still pounding in my chest. I look around. I see nothing. Oh wait! Blood! I had hit it! I look closer. Sprinkles of blood are patterned on top of some leaves. Not much. I look even further. More blood, heavier this time. The trail moves toward the left of where I am standing. I begin a slow walk. I quickly try to reload my rifle. It jams! Excited? Hell yes! I keep walking. More blood splatters; frequent blood splatters. Heavier drops of blood appear. Now clots of blood. Then I see him: He is lying in a pile on top of the dried leaves. He is dead. The heat of the moment passes. My first deer! My first buck! My first season! I begin to breathe more regularly, however raggedly. My heart slows to a softer beat.

"Dad! Dad!" I call. My father finally approaches me from the right side. When he sees the dead deer, the grin on his face is only overshadowed by the bigger grin on my own. He comes up to me and shakes my hand. The deer has a total of only three points, but they are MY three points!

My father immediately takes off my coat. He walks behind me, and he pulls out my shirttail from my pants. He then pulls out his hunting knife. My father cuts off the shirttail! A trophy! His trophy! His son! My deer! I put on my coat. We look over the body for the bullet hole. Not in the shoulders. We locate the bullet nowhere in the body; it is in the neck. I have shot the buck in the neck from thirty yards! Luck? Definitely. Marksmanship? A little. Skill? Absolutely none!

The first thing my father does now is to show me how to gut the deer. We roll the deer onto one side. I take my hunting knife, and I punch it into the stomach area. I cut lengthwise toward the front legs in an uneven fashion. Once I reach the front leg, I then cut the belly open toward the rear leg. With that done, I roll out the guts: heart, liver, stomach, and intestines. Normally we would keep the heart and liver to take home to cook. Today, however, my father just wants to teach me what to do after a kill. Once the body cavity is cleaned out, I cut off the male scent glans behind the knees on each rear leg. When all that was completed, I dry my bloody hands with the dead leaves surrounding me. I take my rifle and show my father the jam.

"Yep!" he exclaims. "Buck fever will do that to you every time!" He pushes down the bullet in the chamber. Once done, he then places his hand in the lever action and closes the breech. He sets the safety lock.

Now it is time to get the buck back to camp. I take out the length of rope from the back of my coat, make a loop in it, and place it around the head of the deer. We begin to drag the deer back to camp, each taking turns pulling it. Time doesn't matter. Space doesn't matter. All that matters is that a father's first son kills his first deer on opening day of his first year of buck season! Life is good. We finally get to camp. We find a sturdy tree limb, sling the rope over it, and hoist the deer into the air to dry. I go inside the cabin; my father goes back out to hunt. My excitement finally disappears, and exhaustion settles all around me. I sleep very hard.

My father and grandfather return to camp after five o'clock, the official state quitting time for hunting. My grandfather shakes my hand with congratulations. He always chews Red Man tobacco. He spits out the wad of tobacco from his mouth. It lands on my boot. Neither my father nor my grandfather had fired a shot all day. They had not even seen any deer. A little later, we break camp, pack up our belongings, lock the cabin door, lower the deer from the tree limb, and pull the deer back to the truck. Once the deer is thrown and stowed into the truck bed, we happily drive back to town. What a day! What an experience! One day that I will remember forever—even as I write this fifty-five years later!

From Home to Homeless—and Salvation

When my wife kicked me out of the house a year ago, I was immediately homeless. My stable and secure life instantly became an unstable, insecure one. The only anchor I had between these two extremes was my "work family."

I had no home with a place to sleep at night. I had $200 in my pocket. I had the clothes on my back and a few other items. I had no bed, no food, no heat, and no future. All I had was this sick, hollow feeling in the pit of my stomach that just wouldn't go away. It left me breathless. I was in total shock.

When I told a few coworkers of my plight, word quickly spread throughout the station that I needed help. The result was overpowering. One girl gave me a room in which I slept for a week. Another girl brought me a real Thanksgiving dinner. Our secretary and her husband opened their spare bedroom to me for a month after my first week's stay was over. She even loaned me money to help me look for an apartment and to set up housekeeping. I felt like Jimmy Stewart in the movie, *It's a Wonderful Life*. What did I ever do to deserve this? Many others gave me hugs, words of encouragement, and related their own personal experiences to me to help ease my pain.

Through diligence on my part and expertise and knowledge on the part of my "work family," I was able to begin to build a new life piece by piece. "God turns mud into flowers" a friend told me. The only way a person can grow, not physically speaking, of course, is to change. Only in the midst of chaos and change can a person learn important life lessons. Every day, stable living provides us with a comfort zone where everything inside that area is happy, complete, and satisfying.

Benjamin Franklin wrote in his epitaph: He wanted to come back "in a new and elegant edition." That's what change and hardship provided: a happier and stronger me when given the chance to grow and bloom amongst kind and loving friends.

Ashamed

I was in eleventh grade in high school. I had been working each summer as a "tender" for my father. He was a bricklayer; my mother was a nurse.

My mother and I went one Saturday into Lewistown to go shopping at McMean's, a quality department store. While my mother went to shop for clothes, I went to the book section. I didn't like to read much, but I did have a fascination with books. My spinster aunt read books from the lending library all the time. liked to look at her collection when I visited. Her books ranged from science fiction to Ayn Rand to Elbert Hubbard's *Little Journeys.*

I had money with me from my recently cashed paycheck. I looked over the selection. Paperback books were not very prevalent in those days so my prospects were only hard-bound books. I looked everything over, and I finally chose Leo Tolstoy's *War and Peace.*

I walked over to the checkout register, paid for the book, and proceeded walk to the parking lot where we always parked the car. My book was in a Mcmean's shopping bag. I got into to the car, and I waited for my mother. In those days, people never locked their cars. I placed the shopping bag on the floor between my legs where I sat. My mother arrived, carrying packages in both hands.

She opened the rear passenger door, threw the packages onto the seat, closed the door, and settled into the driver's seat. We chatted as she started the car, and we headed for home.

Sometime in a lapse of conversation, my mother noticed the package sitting between my legs and asked, "What's in the bag?"

I replied, "A book."

"What book?" she asked.

"*War and Peace*," I replied.

"Why did you buy that?" she asked inquisitively.

"Because I wanted to, and Mrs. Yoder said that it was a really good book." I had Mrs. Yoder as my high school English teacher for four years.

I felt badly. I wanted to hide my package from everyone. My father never read anything because he never completed high school. My mother didn't read much, either. My Aunt Middy read profusely, and my grandmother—my mother's mother—would read stories to us when we were sick and bedridden. I felt ashamed. I felt that I would be reprimanded for buying my first book because I did it myself. I always had to have permission from either parent to do anything. I wanted to hide my book and myself from the world. I lived through it. Looking back, it was my first step toward individualism and independence.

THE ATTIC

I climb the stairs to the attic. I push up the trapdoor at the top of the stairway, blindly reaching for the ribbed metal chain of the light, and I pull it. The single light bulb comes alive, illuminating the dark room and all its contents. I am wearing a white t-shirt, blue jeans, and white Converse sneakers. I crawl over the wooden floor, looking for a smooth spot upon which to sit. The attic is hot and stuffy. There are no air vents, and the heat and humidity are both in the 90s. I am eight years old. The wood on the floor is dark wooden planking such as would be found on the sides of weathered barns. The floor has splinters so I must be very careful where I crawl and where I sit.

My eyes adjust to the room's dimness. I see used lamps, covered boxes, and anything that would normally be stored in a basement. Our house has no basement. The first box I see says "Christmas" written on the outside. When I open it, it contains real aluminum tinsel strands to string around the entire tree. I know that it's real aluminum because some of the spots on the strands are brown with rust. Underneath this come all the lights. The bulbs are large like outdoor lights today. We had four or five strands of these colored lights. Unfortunately, they were all thrown into the box in a haphazard way.

When it was time to unwrap these strands, it took almost an hour to untangle everything! Another box marked "Christmas" contains all the decorations. We have large single colored bulbs. We have small, single-colored bulbs. We have multicolored bulbs. We have a lighted angel for the top of the tree. We have "bubble lights" — lights imitating a candle which when electrified, bubble from the water inside them. We never used candy cane decorations those were to eat. We had single strand aluminum tinsel too. This was placed over the outer branches of the tree to resemble icicles dripping from the tips.

I next spy a two-foot tall figure wrapped in newspaper next to the Christmas boxes. There is a homemade Santa Claus inside. My mother was given it as a little girl. The entire suit is made of red and white real velvet cloth. The hat is also red velvet trimmed with white velvet. The beard is mostly rubbed off. His boots are black fabric stuffed with who knows what upon which he stands. Nothing was plastic; everything was handmade and hand sewn. No matter, though. Every year we unwrap Santa and set him under the tree. We use him as a lure so the "real Santa Claus" will find him on Christmas Eve and drop presents for us for taking care of this Santa throughout the year.

I hear the humming of the wasps outside as they fly to and fro from the nest they made at the arc of the roof. I sweat a lot. The water runs from my forehead and drips onto the wooden floor. It feels like the inside of an oven. Could I actually bake myself up here?

I see a small brown box. It belongs to my mother. It contains her stamp collection from World War II. She never opens it anymore. It is a useless remnant of the past, never to be relived and never to be remembered. Other boxes contain old clothes. Whose, I have no idea. They are just there. Some floor lamps sit in the corner. They do not work. My father stores them here. Why, I do not know. My t-shirt is wet from my neck to my chest from all the sweating I'm doing. The sweat slightly cools my skin, but not much.

I gently crawl over the wooden floor to look into a new box. I know my mother hides our Christmas presents up here. Maybe I can find some! I open the box carefully, trying not to disturb anything so an adult would not be aware that a curious child had searched inside. Toys! I discover toys! Cave men and dinosaurs. All are made of hard rubber, and all are on my Christmas "wish list!" What a find! I pull out a Brontosaurus, with its long neck, long body, and longer tail. I discover a Tyrannosaurus Rex! Boy, is he fierce! I next found a Stegosaurus, with its bony plates along its back and spikes on the tip of its tail. I find a Diplodocus, a water dinosaur with a huge fin covering over half its back and down along its spine. The Triceratops I discover next is really cool-looking! It has its armor-covered hood on its head with the two long horns sticking out from it. The horn atop its nose is extremely frightening.

The cavemen I discover next look awesome! Later, I learned that cavemen and dinosaurs never coexisted together. For an eight-year old boy—who cares? All the cavemen wore pelts around their hips and groin. All were rugged looking —long hair, full beards—and all were very strong and very muscular. One caveman was holding a flint-tipped spear, ready to throw it. Another was carrying a bow with a sheath of arrows on his back. A particularly different one had the caveman holding a heavy rock above his head with outstretched arms, awaiting the right moment to thrust it upon the head of an unsuspecting dinosaur. That's when the spear and bow people would arrive to kill it. If the hunt were successful, it would be raw meat in the cave for supper!

The heat finally gets to me. I feel woozy. I slowly and carefully place all the animals and figures back into the box, close the lid, and adjust it as if it had never been disturbed. I slowly stand up, weave from side-to-side, and make my way over to the light string. I pull the ribbed string, turn around, and descend the stairs. I pull shut the trapdoor and descend the stairs to the second floor of the house. I feel a bit cooler, but the sweat is pouring down my head and neck, completely soaking my t-shirt. My wooziness disappears.

I make my way down all the stairs to the kitchen. There I open the small refrigerator. I reach for the glass milk bottle, pull out the cardboard lid, and drink the cold liquid straight from the bottle. We were never allowed to do this. My mother had just gone to work, and my father had not come home from his bricklaying job. I gulped down the cold milk, replaced the cardboard top, and returned the bottle to its place inside the refrigerator. I walked into the living room, laid down on the couch shoes and all, and quickly fell asleep.

FRIENDSHIP REGAINED

My friend, Corky, is very married, very Mormon, and has five children. This is her story.

> Dear Corky,
> Though our paths through Life will always be separate, we can still hold hands, so to speak, through our friendship.
> Hugs.
> Byrd

Her response was as follows:

> I will always be here with a hand to hold and arms to hug you. You are a wonderful friend. Hugs back.

Corky

Boobs

Lee is my neighbor. She is in her eighties, and she lives upstairs. She has outlived two husbands, and she has had a mild form of leukemia for over twenty years. Sam, short for Samantha, is my apartment manager. She is in her late twenties, and she lives next door.

Sam and I were chatting the other day in her office. In walks Lee. She has been shopping.

After some chit-chat, Lee states, "I can't wait to get home to take this bra off. It hurts my boobies. Of course, I only have one you know. The doctors took the other one."

Lee looked at Sam and continued. "When I was younger, I had pretty good-looking boobies. At least the boys thought so. So did my husband. The boys probably never could tell me what color my eyes were! They weren't looking at them! Look at this," as she placed a breast in each hand," they don't even wiggle the same!" all the while wriggling them up and down and around with her hands.

Sam and I are giggling like school children. Lee continues: "This right one is a prosthesis. It's there just to make me look good. Do you want to touch it, Byrd?"

Shocked, I yelled, "Not on your life, Lee!" as jumped back against the wall behind me with both hands behind my back!

"It's okay. It won't bite!"

Sam is laughing so hard that she's almost crying. I'm laughing, too, though still in shock.

"I was talking to my granddaughter one day, and I asked her if she would like to take it to school for show and tell, but her mother said no."

Sam is now doing eye-rolls, and I'm still standing against the wall with my hands firmly behind my back!

"I don't know what the problem was," Lee said. All Sam and I could do was to continue laughing!

"See you later," Lee said, as she turned around and walked out the door. Sam and I are still bursting at the seams!

"A Trip to "Never-Never Land"
16-23 August 1981

Zaragoza, Spain

"Come fly with us," said Carmen and Luci to their friend Byrd.

"Fine," replied Byrd. "When?"

"The third week in August."

"To where?"

"Asturias, Galicia, and Leon."

"Let's go!" exclaimed Byrd.

Tippy-toe, tippy toe. Out the door and down the sidewalk.

"Shush," whispered Carmen.

"Here's the car," whispered Byrd. "Put everything in here."

They loaded all the luggage, and Carmen and Byrd hopped into the car. Byrd drove over to get Luci and all her baggage.

"Hi, Luci! Are you ready?" said Carmen.

"Si," replied a tired and sleepy Luci.

After all was ready, the three young people drove through a quiet and almost deserted downtown Zaragoza. Nobody seemed to be stirring except our three, young travelers. They proceeded toward the autopista (four-lane highway) to all points north. Byrd did all the driving. Luci immediately gave Carmen her share for expenses and then fell asleep. She was very tired, for she had stayed awake late into the previous night packing and preparing. Byrd was pilot; Carmen was designated primary navigator and treasurer.

The girls had not eaten breakfast, so the first stop was made in Pamplona, the city renowned for its yearly "Running of the Bulls" fiesta. Luci had been to the city a month prior; she explained how it was done, showed us all the streets and the central plaza, and generally provided a guided tour of the entire place. We stopped at a café and ate croissants and drank strong, hot café con leche (coffee with milk). After a visit to "the ladies," the trio again got onto the autopista and proceeded north.

The autopista quickly ended, and the road quickly turned into a two-lane, truck-filled thoroughfare, complete with cart-laden donkeys and other quaint farming modes of travelling.

The trio arrived in the seaside city of San Sebastian at noon. They had no city map, so they drove around looking for a parking place. They eventually found an open spot on the extreme eastern side of the bay. The car was parked, and the three young people began their first stop at "touring."

"Wait, we must change our shoes," said Carmen. We cannot walk in our dress shoes."

"I must get my sweater," stated Luci.

"Are you ready yet?" asked Byrd.

"Si, si" replied the girls.

"Let's go then. To where?"

"Along the beach and around the bay," said Carmen.

"Look at all the people," exclaimed Byrd. I don't see many topless beach bathers!"

"No," explained Luci, "this city is so much more conservative than Sitges. Oh, look! There are three now!"

"I see," replied Byrd, but he really did not see anything. Just three topless females lying face down on a towel. Rats!

"The last time I was here, I had a picture taken of me on this bridge," stated Carmen. "I'll take another one today," said Byrd.

"No, indeed! My hair is a mess!"

San Sebastian is built along a coast shaped like to U's joined together. The beach is very large. The city is located on the northeastern coast of the Spanish section of the Cantabrian Sea, next to the French border. It is a popular resort area and vacation spa for both French and Spanish tourists.

The day itself was hot, and the humidity was high. Visibility for picture taking was limited, due to the extreme haze layer. The beaches and the city were extremely crowded because it was the height of holiday season for Spain. The city itself was old. One could definitely see that the beach was the main attraction.

The trio walked out to the farthest point of the peninsula adjoining the two bays. Byrd took several pictures, including two of the girls. These photographs were snapped at great risk to the photographer since the high humidity made each girl's hair straighten into lifeless shapes. The girls' appearance—especially the ways their hair looked—was extremely important to them throughout the entire trip (or so Byrd thought)!

"I am hungry!" Luci declared.

"Oh," exclaimed Byrd. "Where would you like to eat? Here on the beach or somewhere in the city?"

"Not here; in the city," stated Carmen.

"Look how far we've walked though," declared Byrd. I'll bet it's at least two kilometers. We still have to go back to the car!"

"We go," stated the girls in unison.

So the three retraced their steps around the bay and returned to the car. Tired and hungry, they began driving again.

"Which way?"

"To the right. The same way as we walked."

"Okay."

"It's five kilometers total that we walked! Oh no! A dead-end street!" exclaimed Byrd. "Now how do I turn the car around in this place?"

Using a gentle and cautious maneuver, Byrd got the car turned around, and once again Byrd drove into the center of the city.

"Where can we park?"

"Keep driving. We will look for a place for...Stop! Stop! We will park here in the garage. It's better."

"Okay."

"I lost my stomach. I am so hungry that my front is touching my back, and so I lost my stomach! I want a big dinner."

"Here's a restaurant."

"No, is too crowded."

"Look at that one! The line goes clear to the end of the block!"

"I am very hungry, but I can eat somewhere else. People are crazy to stand in line like that."

"How about this one? This has no people standing outside."

"Oh, is crowded here. Is only at the bar, though. We go around the corner."

"What? This is the line waiting for the restaurant to open. Unbelievable!"

Back around the corner through the mob of hungry, waiting people they went. Outside once again, they proceeded to look for a restaurant in which to eat. Ten minutes later, Carmen spied a two-start hotel/restaurant. "We will try this," she said.

Through the door and up the stairs they walked. "Is nice."

"There is a table. We take that one."

The waitress brought a menu. There were two selections from which to choose: paella and steak or chicken and soup. The girls chose paella and steak since Byrd could only read a limited amount of Spanish. Agua sin gas (natural mineral water) and a basket of pan (bread) were delivered.

"I go to the ladies; then we eat," said Carmen.

Tick, tick, tick. Ten minutes, twenty minutes, thirty minutes.

"I go to 'the ladies, too. Maybe we eat when I return," sighed Luci.

Tick, tick, tick. Forty minutes, fifty minutes, one hour.

"Where is our food?" cried Luci. "I blow away soon!"

The waitress was asked about the food, and she said, "Manana (tomorrow)!"

Tick, tick, tick...fifteen more minutes passed.

"At last! Food!" shouted Luci.

Salad, paella, steak, and ice cream: All was brought, but not all was eaten.

"Is too much food. I walk very far today. I am too tired to eat it all."

"Ugh. Stop! No more steak, please. I'm full. No, Carmen, don't want all of your paella."

Lunch was finished—finally. By this time, it was approaching four o'clock.

"Do you like to stay overnight in Santander?" asked Carmen to Byrd.

"It's fine with me," he replied.

Onto the autopista once again, heading west. First through Bilbao, where the autopista ended. Then on a two-lane road through Castro-Urdiales. Then Laredo, and finally into Santander at seven o'clock.

"Look, a five-star hotel. Would you like to stay there?" asked Byrd.

"No, is too expensive. We park here first," stated Carmen. "We walk around the bend..."

No, stop it's too far to walk. We drive farther into town and along the beach."

"Stop here. Can you park the car in this place?"

"Yes," said Byrd. "We'll fit."

Byrd parked the car right next to the beach and only a stone's throw away from the primary tourist area. Santander was also crowded with people, and the heat and humidity were just as bad as in San Sebastian.

"We have several hotels to look for a room. It's late, and I think we should find a place in which to sleep," Byrd suggested.

"Okay," replied the girls.

Walk, walk, walk. "No, I'm sorry. We have no rooms." Walk, walk, walk. "No hay camas."

"Completo." More walking. By this time, the three were terribly tired, uncomfortably hot, and in need of a room. The time was past eight o'clock.

"What about this four-start hotel?" asked Byrd. "I would rather have a bed. Don't worry about the expenses."

"Okay, we look here."

"Do you have two rooms, one double and one single?" asked Carmen.

"No," replied the man at the reception desk. "We only have two double rooms."

"We take them," said Carmen.

The information cards were filled in, Luci produced her ID card, and, finally, the weary travelers lumbered to the elevator in search of their rooms.

"Look at this! Three beds! We were cheated. Look at the size of this room. Is huge!"

"Let's see what the other room is like."

"Si. We do that."

Up to the third floor the trio climbed—to look at the second room.

"Oh, this is nice, too, but it still has two beds! What are we going to do with five beds!!" "Well, we could sleep in all five of them!"

"Ha! Ha! Ha! No, will never work. We think of something. For now, we go to our rooms and take nice hot showers."

"Sounds great! I'm too tired to do anything. A shower and a bed seem tremendous."

The trio went back down to the second floor. It was decided that Luci would take the room with the three beds, and Byrd and Carmen would sleep in the other.

So ended the first day of the vacation. {Sunday, 16 August)

The next morning, the three gathered down in Luci's room at ten o'clock. The first thing they did was to check out of the hotel, load the car with their bags, and look for a place for breakfast. They went around the corner from the hotel to a place Luci had found the night before. Luci had gone out for several drinks after her shower to make her sleep better. After a short walk, they found the restaurant they sought. The girls ate omelets, tostados, and drank cafe con leche. Byrd also had coffee along with a ham and cheese sandwich.

Carmen had called a friend of hers, Maripi, the evening before. The two had spent time in London together prior to Carmen's going to Dublin to learn English. A time was set for 1630 for a visit of the two at a café along the beach. So what to do until then....

"Come, we look for Maripi's house."

Up a hill; down a hill; around a corner. Up, down around, and almost back to where they had begun. During all the walking, the girls talked about Maripi. Luci also related a story about her ex-boyfriend whom she had almost married. The story was funny in some parts but, overall, it was very sad. The search proved fruitless; the house was not found. In disappointment, the group headed downtown to see the sights and to window shop.

Santander was a pretty town, and the girls truly enjoyed it. The walk lasted well into the afternoon. The walk lasted so long, though, that they finally had to sit down on a park bench and literally catch their breath. The day was warm, although overcast, and there was a slight breeze. The humidity was still horrid, however.

The rest was refreshing. At three o'clock, the trio began their return walk to the cafe to meet Maripi. They found the appointed spot, bought something each to drink, and waited for Carmen's friend.

"Where is Maripi? She said she would be here," said Luci.

"I will go around the corner and look around." said Carmen. Around the corner Carmen went.

"Maripi!"

"Carmen!"

They hugged each other and returned to the table where Luci and Byrd sat. Introductions. Chat, chat, chat, chat. Wedding pictures of Maripi. Chat, chat, chat, chat. Maripi's London pictures. Chat, chat. Byrd was bored; everything spoken was in Spanish Here comes Maripi's husband.

"Buenos tardes."

Chat, chat, chat.

"Where are you going tonight?"

"To Oviedo."

"That is a very long drive. It is almost seven o'clock now. You must be leaving soon."

"Si, si."

"But first can we take pictures of everyone?"

"Okay. Fine."

Snap, snap, click, click.

"Nice to meet you, Byrd. I hope next we meet is at your and Carmen's wedding!" exclaimed Maripi.

"Oh, no! Not again!" cried Byrd. "I think I've heard this before."

Everyone laughed.

"Adios. Hasta luego."

On the road again heading west. Fully fueled. The road is bad, and there are many trucks. Progress is terribly slow.

"We should get to Oviedo by eleven o'clock. That's late, but you said, Luci, that you called your friend," said Byrd.

"Si. Alberto will be waiting for us," Luci replied.

More driving. It is beginning to get dark.

"I am hungry," stated Carmen.

"Okay," said Byrd. "At the next restaurant I see, we'll stop and get something to eat."

A little while later, Byrd turned the car into the parking lot of a small restaurant. Bocadillos (sandwiches) were ordered along with agua sin gas. Then it was back into the car and back onto the road.

"We'll be in Oviedo between eleven o'clock and midnight," said Byrd.

"Alberto will be waiting," replied Luci.

"I hope so; I'm very tired."

More road. More trucks. Darkness. Slowly, slower, slow. Luci slept. Carmen watched the road and occasionally talked to Byrd. Longer. Ten o'clock. One hundred kilometers. Eleven o'clock. One hundred fifty kilometers. Rattle, rattle, bump, bump. Bad road.

"Finally! Oviedo!" exclaimed Byrd. "I'm not driving anymore. I quit!"

"You are very tired," Carmen whispered to Byrd. "We find a bed, and then we sleep."

"I hope so."

Luci was awakened so the she would know they had arrived in Oviedo.

"Stop by a telephone. I will call Alberto," whispered Luci through a yawn.

"Here's one," said Byrd.

The call was made, and Luci came back smiling.

"We meet him at Plaza America. Now we look for it."

"Where to, Carmen?" Byrd asked.

"I think this way," replied Carmen.

Five minutes later.

"Stop! Stop!" shouted Carmen, "We are here!"

"Are you sure?" asked Luci.

"Si."

Five minutes. Ten minutes. Fifteen minutes.

"Where is Alberto?"

"I do not know. He must be here by now."

"Are you sure this is the right place?"

"Si, is the right place. He said Plaza America."

Twenty minutes. Thirty minutes.

"I go look for him," said Luci.

Later.

"There they come, Carmen," said Byrd. I'll bet he was waiting on the other side of the plaza!"

"He was waiting on the other side of the plaza!" exclaimed a slightly embarrassed Luci.

Into the car.

"Drive this way," said Alberto.

"Do you have rooms for us?" asked Carmen.

"I think I do. I have not made reservations," replied Alberto sheepishly.

Midnight. Into the hotel. No rooms. Around the corner. No rooms. Up the street and around the corner. Into another hotel. This one is a two-star.

"Si, we have two rooms," stated the manager.

"We look at them," said Carmen.

Up the elevator to the fifth floor. The rooms were inspected. "We take them," Carmen sighed sleepily.

The rooms turned out to be nothing more than a place to sleep. The beds were small doubles. There was only one small closet (with no hangers), one window, and scant furniture. There was absolutely no ventilation; the rooms were terribly hot. It was like we were in the hotel attic! The bathrooms were ugly. They were small, crowded, and unaccountably unclean. But the travelers were extremely tired; all they wished to do was sleep.

Sleep, sleep...but sleep does not come. It was extremely hot and terribly uncomfortable. They were all restless. After a long, uncomfortable night, sleep closed our travelers' eyes a few hours prior to sunrise. (Monday, 17 August)

Morning. Ten thirty.

"Ugh. I feel terrible," grudged Byrd. "How do you feel?"

"Very tired," sighed a quiet Carmen.

"Should we get up?"

"Yes. Is late."

Morning produced four, very grumpy and very tired individuals. Alberto went to work so the other three looked for breakfast.

"Café con leche, orange juice, and manzanilla (apple juice), por favor."

"Muy bien."

"You aren't eating much, Luci," stated Byrd. "Why?"

"I was sick all night. Alberto and I went out for drinks, and it was terrible. I lost my stomach four times. I just drink manzanilla," whispered Luci.

"Do you have aspirin or anything?"

"I take a seltzer. I be well soon."

After breakfast the three began to window shop. All three were too tired to walk very far so the window shopping quickly ended. All were disinterested. All each wished to do was sleep, but no one said a word. It was just too obvious.

"Is almost one o'clock," sighed Luci. "We meet Alberto to take him home. We go to Plaza America again."

"Okay."

Waiting. One o'clock comes and goes. More waiting. One-fifteen. "Where is Alberto, Luci?"

"I do not know. He said he would meet us here. I go look for him." Luci was very exasperated—as well as upset.

"Not again!" exclaimed Byrd. "We didn't!"

"Yes, we did," Luci replied unabashedly. "He was waiting on the other side of the plaza!"

"Hi, Alberto!"

"Buenos."

"Where to?"

"In the car. I direct," Alberto stated emphatically.

Through downtown traffic, around the city, and onto a main thoroughfare. Out of the city and up into the hills.

"Stop here," declared Alberto.

Byrd stopped and parked the car. They had arrived at an old monastery that was popular with visiting tourists. There was little to see for the building was completely boarded shut. Byrd took many pictures though. Even Alberto agreed to have his picture taken with Luci. It was nice and quiet there and very relaxing. They finished their visit and began their ride back down the hill.

"Are you thirsty, Byrd?" asked Carmen.

"Yes, very much so," replied a very tired Byrd.

"We stop at this café," stated Alberto. "This café serves excellent cider. It is the pride of Asturias!"

Two, tall bottles were ordered by Alberto. He paid for both of them. The cider was freshly made so it had to be poured in a special manner. The glass was held at the hip. The bottle was held at head level. As the cider was poured, it was directed to hit the upper lip of the glass so the glass filled slowly. This process mixed the raw ingredients in the homemade cider, as well as aerating the liquid. The technique was quite unique, but much cider was spilled in the process. The cider was excellent! It also was very intoxicating if one drank too much. The happy group consumed four bottles in all. Everyone felt a slight tingle from all the alcohol.

The sun broke through the overcast, and Oviedo city could be dimly seen in the distance, though not much could be clearly distinguished. The city was large, but not much else was clear. The warm sun, the cool breeze, and the intoxicating cider began to make all members of the group very drowsy.

"Is time we go. We take Alberto home."

"Okay."

They traveled to the town of Trubia. There they bought freshly made bocadillos, grapes, apples, and agua sin gas. They next drove around the block and let out Alberto at his designated place.

"Adios, Alberto."

"Adios. I see you soon, Luci, in Zaragoza. I call you. Gracias. Hasta luego."

"Adios. Hasta luego."

Later, Luci stated: "I hope he does not visit soon. I do not know what to do if he comes to Zaragoza."

"Why, Luci?" asked Byrd. "Do you have too many hot dates already?"

"No, I do not. I just will not know what to do with him," Luci admonished.

"Don't worry, Luci. If he doesn't love you, we still do," Byrd said energetically. "We'll take care of you."

"Gracias. You are very kind."

Equipped with food, water, and fruit, the drive continued. Up hills, down hills, around hills. Fast, slow, stopped. Trucks, cars, and mule carts. Towns, cities, resorts, farms. Mountains, meadows, and an occasional river to bridge. Still traveling west. Finally, Luarca.

"Where are we?" asked Byrd.

"Luarca," Carmen quietly relied.

"Is a beautiful place," declared an excited Luci. "I like very much."

"I do, too," Byrd said.

"We park and look," stated Carmen.

"Great."

"I like very much. Do you want to stay here tonight?"

"Si."

"That's the best answer I've heard all day. Where to?"

"We walk and look."

Byrd parked the car, and they began to walk. Small houses, tiny cafes, a natural cove, and a quiet and lovely evening. There were many people and many fishing boats. It was a natural resort area. Solitude.

"I'm sorry. We have no room."

"No hay camas."

"Si, we have rooms. We only have single rooms. How many beds? Three? No, we have no doubles or singles. We do, however, have one double and one single in the same room. That is all that remains. Take it or leave it."

The reception desk was at a two-star hotel. The trio realized they had little choice of where they were to sleep. They were inexorably tired.

"We take it," Carmen sighed.

"Here is my ID," stated a sleepy Luci.

"Follow me, and I will show you where you will sleep," said the hotel clerk.

"We follow you."

Around the corner and up the hill went the four.

"Here is the house. The room is toward the rear."

"Ooh. Look at this!'

"Is beautiful!"

"All I want to do is sleep."

"Is clean, bright... I like very much."

The room was clean...and very nice. It contained two beds, a large dresser with closet, nice furniture, and a small sink—including glasses. The bathroom was communal, but it was big and the water was very hot. The beds were comfortable, and the surroundings were quiet.

With all in order in the room, the three began a tour of the little town. It was very quaint. Located on the end of a natural cove, Luarca was nestled beneath high cliffs and beautiful surroundings. It was, therefore, a natural tourist attraction. Many fishing boats aligned the wharf. A few hardy sailors still could be seen out among the rolling waves of the Cantabrian Sea. The air was refreshing. The group was so tired, though, that they just enjoyed the scenery and the pleasant solitude of the rolling ocean. They were too tired to eat much, though they did stop and get something. The item they desired most was water. It had been a long day due to lack of sleep the night before. The cider they had drunk had not helped much either.

Finally, weariness overcame them, and they could walk no further. They ventured back to the hotel and prepared for bed. The hot shower was a welcome relief. Since everyone was sleeping in the same room, mutual accommodations were established. Eventually, everyone was tucked neatly into bed, and the light was about ready to be turned out. Until Luci asked...

"Will you tell me a bedtime story, Byrd? I cannot sleep without a story!"

"A story! What can I tell? I don't know anything suitable for the two of you," Byrd responded.

"Tell us something. Anything."

"Alright, let me think. Umm. I could tell you a Christmas story if you wish."

"No, is not Christmas."

"Well, how about the story of 'Peter Pan'? Have you ever heard that?"

"No, tell it to us."

"Well, once upon a time (the girls laughed quietly at that), there was a family called the Darling family. It consisted of Master Darling, Mistress Darling, Wendy the daughter, and her two younger brothers. They also had a dog called Nana. She kept the very young children..."

"...and so Wendy grew up, and every year Peter Pan returned to take Wendy's children back to 'Never-Never Land.' Nana and Tinkerbell died. But Peter Pan never, ever did grow up."

"Is a sad story. But you tell it well. I liked it."

"I heard it in Spanish before, but you tell it better. Thank you very much. I can sleep now."

"Goodnight, Luci."

"Not Luci. Nana! I like Nana!"

"Goodnight, Nana."

"Woof! Goodnight."

"Whom would you like to be then, Carmen?"

"Wendy."

"Goodnight, Wendy."

"Goodnight, Peter Pan!" laughed both girls simultaneously.

"Ha, ha, ha! Goodnight!"

(Tuesday, 18 August)

"Good morning. How did you sleep?"

"Very good. And you?"

"Very good."

"Hi, Luci! Are you awake?"

"Si. I am very hungry this morning."

"Don't worry; Carmen and I will help you look for your stomach!"

"Gracias." Then everyone laughed.

Down the hill and around the corner they went. They found a nice, clean café, ordered breakfast, and just watched the other tourists with their early morning preparations. After they had eaten, Carmen wanted to look for the post office. The next day was her father's birthday, and she wanted to send him a birthday greeting. Off they went in search of the post office.

"Look, Carmen!" Luci exclaimed in surprise. "Empanadas!"

"Muy bien. Do you want some?"

"Si."

"And you, Byrd. Do you want a Spanish empanada?"

"What are they?"

"They are cakes filled with fish. They are baked in long pans, and then cut into small squares. They are very delicious."

"Sounds good to me, but we just ate."

"You will like them anyway."

"Why not!"

Three large slices of empanada were procured from the store keeper. Satisfied, the travelers continued toward the post office.

"Yum, yum. Those were very good," said a happy and fully contented Luci.

"Nana would eat anything!" interjected Byrd.

"Is true! That is why I watch my weight all the time."

"Yes, you watch it go up!" laughed Byrd and Carmen. "When will Nana be grown up?"

"Nana does not grow up in 'Never-Never Land'." Luci retorted happily. "I like the way I am."

"We do too," replied a gratified and amiable Byrd. Carmen just smiled.

They found the post office eventually, and Carmen sent her birthday message to her father. They finished their short tour and went to the hotel office to pay for the rooms. Once again in the car, the group continued their journey westward toward La Coruna.

On and on they went. They drove past the resort and town of Ribadeo, along the winding and sometimes rocky coast, through Vivero, and toward their next stop, El Ferrol del Caudillo. This entire trip was spent passing beautiful green trees, rolling hillsides, small farms, and occasional glimpses of an ice-gray sea. Through the entire area, the road they traveled wound around and around like a snake. The three people felt happy throughout the long drive because they were all well rested, well fed, and anxious for more adventures.

They finally arrived in the city of El Ferrol del Caudillo in early afternoon. They drove into the central city, through a mistaken turn, they drove down through many narrow, dirty, and extremely crowded streets. The city was not that nice.

"Do not stop here." Carmen said. "This is a very dirty place; I do not like it very much."

"Si, drive somewhere else," Luci responded. "We see some other place."

"Which way, Wendy?" Byrd asked. He secretly wanted to drive to La Coruna and find a room. He was beginning to get tired of driving so much. Along the road to El Ferrol, they passed the one thousand kilometer mark on the odometer.

"I don't know," replied Carmen.

"Which way? To La Coruna or south?" asked an impatient Byrd.

"To Betanzos," answered Carmen.

"Okay. Just help me get out of this city."

"Si. We can do that."

They found the right road down to Betanzos, but it led them back through the center of El Ferrol Caudillo…and through the public squared.

"Look! Look! There is Franco!" cried an excited Luci.

What Luci had seen was a gigantic metal cast of Generalisimo Francisco Franco, Spain's deceased dictator and the main figurehead in the shaping of modern Spain. The Generalisimo sat astride a large stallion. His stature posed a very formidable sight. The girls began to laugh.

"What's so funny?" Byrd asked.

No response. Just more laughter.

"What's happening? What are you two laughing about?"

"Is a big statue." laughed Luci.

"Si," replied a jolly Carmen. "Too big!"

More laughter. The girls were beginning to roll over themselves from the thoughts they were having.

"Will you two please tell me what's going on?" cried Byrd in complete exasperation.

"Si. Ha, ha, ha. Franco was a very short man! Ha, ha, ha, ha, ha! The statue makes him look like a giant!" giggle Camren.

"And he is so proud and straight on top of his horse!" laughed Luci. "He was not that way at all when he lived."

"He wasn't?" questioned Byrd.

"No, not at all. He was a very short guy with a very dumpy figure. The statue is not at all a good description of him. It makes him look bigger than he really was." explained Luci through her tears. "Is very funny!"

"Ha, ha, ha! I agree," laughed Byrd, finally understanding the joke. El Ferrol del Caudillo was Franco's birthplace,

They finally found their way out of the town and headed toward Betanzos. The day was still overcast, and the air seemed to hang all around like a blanket. There was no wind. The trio drove south in silence, except for Luci's offering Byrd and Carmen an apple or an occasional grape still left over from Trubia.

They arrived in Betanzos, and the initial impression the girls had was one of disappointment. The town was not at all appealing, and it too was very dirty. The gray sky only dampened their spirits further. They parked the car and began to walk. They found a little bar, and all ordered café con leche.

"I cannot understand a word they are talking," exclaimed Luci about the customers around them.

"It is all in Galician, and I know nothing at all!"

"Now you know how I feel sometimes when I can't understand your Spanish!" explained Byrd. "It is exactly the same circumstance."

"Si, I understand," Luci replied. Carmen also understood; her eyes expressed it.

They finished their coffees and continued their walk. They passed through a bridge filled with people watching men in kayaks float down the river. They eventually made it to the center of the city. A fair was being held there: Rides, candy, and other attractions were to be seen and enjoyed if one wished to participate.

"Let's leave. I don't like this place, either," Carmen stated matter-of-factly.

"I don't like it either," Luci said flatly.

Back on the road again, the group headed west to La Coruna. This is the largest city in northwestern Spain. It is also the capital of the province. It was only a short drive before the car was in the middle of traffic in the central downtown area. They had just stopped for a traffic light when...

"Buenos. Are you tourists?" a stranger asked from the side of the road.

"Si, si."

"I can show you my private dwelling. It is on the other side of the city. Are you interested?" he asked.

This entire conversation was in Spanish so Byrd had no idea whom this man was. All that he could fathom was he was elderly, friendly, and very persuasive. After a short discussion between the girls, Carmen finally replied, "Si."

The man got into the back of the car with Luci.

"What's this, Carmen?" Byrd asked just as the traffic light turned green. "Who's he?"

"He has offered to show me his residence. He has empty rooms for us to sleep in tonight. Is okay."

"Oh."

Byrd followed the instructions given by the man through the interpretation of the girls. They passed the ocean front, the docks, and arrived at an apartment complex high on a hill overlooking the city.

"Stop. We are here," Carmen stated.

Byrd parked the car, and the three young people followed the man into the apartment.

"Is exactly like the last time I was here," explained Luci. "The people of this city are very friendly. They ask tourists to spend the night in their private homes. They walk the streets, just like as happened to us, to see if visitors need a place to sleep. Is very different from any other part of Spain."

"I can see that," nodded Byrd in agreement.

The apartment complex where the man had led them was extremely new and very clean. The rooms themselves were nice, comfortable, but rather small.

"We have a choice." stated Carmen. "We can sleep in one room with two beds, or we can we can all sleep in one bed! Which do you want to do?"

"I don't care," declared Luci.

"Well," Byrd said, "since Spanish beds are on the small side, we might have trouble all sleeping in one bed. I would rather have the two beds; we've already lived in that situation before. How do you two feel?"

"Is fine," Carmen nodded.

"Si," replied Luci. "Is okay."

Luci then signed for the room, and the trio transported all their luggage from the car to it. The beds were adequate, the furnishings nice, but still everything was on the small side. There were two, big bathrooms to use, however, and the water was nice and hot for their showers.

After settling in, the three headed toward the central plaza—window shopping, talking, and thoroughly enjoying themselves and the new sights around them. They looked at shoes, clothes, more shoes, jewelry, and bars. The city was fascinating. Many stores had beautiful displays, and all were brightly illuminated.

They found a little restaurant and ate a small meal. Fish and its accessories was the primary cuisine. The restaurant was small, but clean, and the food was good.

It was quite dark by this time so all the store displays in gallant prominence. Everything looked so pretty—and so very expensive. As they walked along the main street, someone called.

"Hola, Luci!"

"Oh, my, look Carmen," Luci exclaimed in surprise. "We meet these two in Sitges."

It was true: The two young men who had stopped the girls to say hello were already known. Carmen and Luci had met them on the beach at Sitges over Fourth of July weekend. It was a real coincidence to haphazardly meet them on the street in a city way up in northwestern Spain. After a short conversation, the young men left, and our group continued with their walking and their window shopping.

"I cannot believe it!" Luci exclaimed in excitement. "How could we ever meet them again? Is unbelievable."

"True."

It was getting late, and the girls were tiring very fast. They turned their steps around and proceeded toward their room.

"Does anyone know where we are?" Luci asked. "I am lost."

"We are just down the hill and around the corner from our apartment. See, over there is the plaza we crossed, and that is the ocean," Byrd indicated.

"You are right." Luci agreed. "You are a good navigator!"

"No, Luci, you are just a bad dog!"

"Humph," said Luci as she stalked away from Byrd and Carmen, but she was smiling. "Bad dog! I never go with you to Never-Never Land again!"

"Okay, you can stay at home next time."

"No. I like flying with Peter Pan!"

"I do, too," Carmen laughed.

Halfway up the hill to where their apartment was located, Luci exclaimed, "Can we sit and rest? I am very tired." They all relaxed on a bench, and Luci smoked a cigarette.

"Can you tell me another bedtime story?" Luci asked Byrd. "Only a short one this time."

"Sure! Let's see. Umm. Have you ever heard the story about *The Tortoise and the Hare*?" Byrd asked.

"What is a tortoise?" asked Carmen.

"What is a hare?" asked Luci. "I do not know that word."

"Tortoise...ah, tortuga. Comprende?"

"Si, si," replied the girls.

"Hare is a rabbit. Uh, what is the word for rabbit?" "Conejo."

"Si, conejo," Byrd stated. "Once upon a time, there was a tortoise and a hare, and they were going to have a race...So the moral of the story is that if you keep trying and do the best you possibly can, you will win the race."

"I like very much," Carmen whispered sleepily.

"You are a good storyteller," Luci yawned.

"Come, it's time to go. I'm terribly tired."

"Si, si."

Up the hill they went, and once again they found the apartment and the rooms they had been given. Preparations for bed were quickly made, and soon all three heads were safely nestled under the bed covers. The light was quickly turned out.

"Goodnight, Wendy! Goodnight, Nana!"

"Goodnight, Peter Pan!" (Wednesday, 19 August)

"What time is it?"

"Ten thirty. Is late."

"Do you want to get up?"

"Yes."

"No. Nana is still sleeping."

"Let's get up."

"No. Nana wants to sleep."

"Si, we get up."

The car was packed; the bill was paid; and once again the three were on the road. They had finally reached the west coast of Spain—and the Atlantic Ocean—so their direction changed to that of south.

An autopista was built from La Coruna to Santiago de Compostela, their next stop. And that was only sixty kilometers away! It was an easy drive. Halfway along the autopista, everyone got hungry for they had no breakfast. Byrd pulled off the road at the Ordenes service area. They ate ham bocadillos and drank café con leche. Thirty kilometers later, they drove into the city of Santiago de Compostela.

Santiago has a main attraction where tourists from all over the world come to see: The cathedral. It lies at the end of a long journey (the El Camino Way), which many pilgrims traverse each year in their religious quests. It sits at the end of the road called The Way of Saint James. It is truly beautiful. The outside is adorned with three large facades. The interior of the building is constructed in the shape of a cross. The inside is exquisitely magnificent.

Our travelers then drove into the heart of the city. The first parking place they found happened to be in front of an apartment that advertised "hay camas." They went inside, inquired with the landlady, and looked at the two rooms shown. Santiago also has a large university—ergo, a large student population. The city provided many habitations for the students. The rooms the group saw were two such habitations. The rooms were plain, but they were adequate.

"We take," Carmen said.

After they had stored their luggage, they went outside and began exploring. First they walked up a hill and down around through a small square. They stopped for coffee. Then they continued their search for the cathedral, whom all three dearly wanted to see.

They walked and walked. Eventually, they found the place for which they sought. The cathedral sat before a very large stone plaza surrounded by two government buildings and a five-star hotel. All were old, and all were made of stone. All were very beautiful, and their aesthetic aura was sensational. The tour was quickly finished. Carmen and I each lit a candle at the main altar and said a prayer. Byrd took many pictures of the cathedral, and he also managed to get a quick shot of the girls.

Not much time was spent around the cathedral after the tour ended. They walked down into the central part of town to window shop. They passed many shops which sold religious paraphernalia. It also seemed that all the roads around the cathedral led down the hill to a central shopping square composed of bars, shops, restaurants, and food vendors. The area was quite nice; it was also filled with many people and was very active with business.

"Look, Carmen!" exclaimed Byrd.

"A Spanish musician playing bagpipes! I can't believe it!"

Byrd raised his camera to take a picture, but the man stopped playing and walked over to where Byrd was standing. He began to talk to Byrd in accelerated Spanish, but Byrd understood not a word.

"He wants one hundred pesetas," Luci explained. "I don't have any. Could you lend me some?"

Byrd paid the money he requested. The musician quickly pocketed it, and he began to play the same tune he had played before. Byrd then took the man's picture. The group then continued into the busy square.

"Look, Carmen!" Luci exclaimed in surprise, "Empanadas!"

"We get some," Carmen replied.

"I think the store is closed," interjected Byrd.

"No," cried Luci, "and I was hungry for empanadas!"

"Me, too," sighed Carmen.

They continued their tour. More shops, more windows, and much more walking. Down the hill; up the hill. Down a new road. At the square again! Back up the hill to the cathedral. Down past the shop with the empanadas.

"Is still closed," Luci hungrily stated. Byrd could hear both Luci's and Carmen's stomachs growling for the entire walk!

It was well past noon by now, and the sun finally broke through the cloud layer. The heat felt good, and all three people got drowsy.

"Are you thirsty?" Carmen asked Byrd.

"Yes."

They stopped at an outside café and sat next to a table that was fully illuminated by the sun. The warmth felt good, for it was the first real sunshine they had experienced in all their recent travels. Each person ordered drinks, sat back to enjoy the sunshine, and just watched all the people. They watched Frenchmen, an occasional German, and many students. Spaniards flocked by in hundreds. Even a stray dog or two trotted past them.

"No, Luci," commented Byrd, "that isn't Nana!"

They watched a little while longer.

"Let's walk," Byrd said emphatically.

All three got up to go when Luci exclaimed: "Look, look! The store is open!"

"We buy some empanadas," Carmen laughed excitedly.

They bought three large slices of empanadas.

"This is much better than the one we had before."

"Si. Is much better."

"True."

Their walk continued. They went into a nearby park and sat down again in front of a water-filled pond and a nice statue. Luci smoked a cigarette, and Carmen rested against Byrd's arm. Suddenly, Luci started to giggle. It was contagious, and Carmen began to giggle too. Soon both girls were laughing hilariously.

"Is that time of day again," Luci giggled.

"I can't—ha, ha, ha—help myself," Carmen laughed.

"We must be in Never-Never land." Byrd said. "There many strange things happen."

"Si, we are in Never-Never Land, and you are a real Peter Pan!" laughed Luci.

"I don't know about being Peter Pan," Byrd said, "but I will take you anywhere you want to go!"

"You have already!" exclaimed Carmen. "We are now in Santiago de Compostela! We have traveled many kilometers throughout Galicia."

"That's true," Byrd replied.

Suddenly Luci took out all the make-up, mascara, and lipstick she had in her purse.

"What are you doing?" asked Byrd.

"I am ugly. I make myself pretty again," Luci commented.

"I do, too," said Carmen.

So for the next forty-five minutes, Byrd watched both Luci and Carmen make their faces and fix their hair. It was a very enlightening experience! At least for Byrd, anyway. After the "make up session" came to an end, they all resumed the walk through the park.

The park itself was very big. It adjoined the square, and at its highest point. It overlooked the campus of Santiago University. The park was beautiful. It contained many trees, both deciduous and coniferous, as well as many fountains, statues, a church at the top and myriads of flowers. They could even see the upper half of the cathedral from one vantage point! Everyone enjoyed themselves. It was late in the day now so the trio started their walk back toward their rooms.

"Are you hungry, Byrd?" asked Carmen.

"Not really."

"But you can eat anyway?"

"Yes, I can eat anyway. Are you hungry?"

"I am hungry."

"Okay, we'll find a place to eat."

"Is early."

"Okay, we'll wait then."

"No, we eat now."

On their return, they found a suitable restaurant. It was open, but because it was only six o'clock in the evening, there were no customers in it. Carmen, Luci, and Byrd had the entire place to themselves! They made the best of it too! They each ordered large dinners: salads, fish, and ice cream. To complete the meal, Luci ordered a large bottle of white Pazo wine. It tasted excellent.

"I must buy some of this wine for gifts before we leave here," declared Luci.

"It's made in Orense, Luci. You can wait until we get there to buy some," said Byrd.

"Okay, I do that then."

They finished their dinners. Each was fully satiated. They were very happy.

"We look for a telephone when we go back," said Carmen. "I call Javier." Javier was Carmen's brother, and he lived in Leon. The three would pass through Leon on their return to Zaragoza. They left the restaurant, began to walk back toward their rooms, and looked for a telephone booth in the meantime. Carmen eventually located a phone, made her call, and returned. "He will be waiting for us when we get to Leon," she said. "He will also have hotel reservations ready."

Back in their rooms, they showered and went to bed early. Their next day would entail much driving. (Thursday, 20 August)

"Buenos dias."

"Buenos dias."

Out the door and across the street for a light breakfast. The day was perfect: bright sunshine, no wind, and not a cloud in the sky. A little more window shopping. They went into a clothing store. Luci saw some blouses she liked, but all the ones she modeled were too large. She bought nothing. They next explored a department store. There Carmen bought Byrd a little book in which to write their story of the trip, and Byrd found two copies of *Peter Pan* written in Spanish. He gave each girl a copy of the illustrated book. They loved the gifts; it was more than apropos. Their shopping soon ended; it was time to drive.

South to Pontevedra they journeyed. There was no autopista, but the road was just as good. They spent no time at all in Pontevedra.

"I want to see Marin and the island resort of La Toja," said Carmen.

"Okay. Which way do we go: north to La Toja or south to Marin?" Byrd asked.

"I don't know."

"Well, make up your mind, Carmen. Which way?"

"Does not matter."

"In that case, why not go north to Grove and La Toja? Then we can return south through Pontevedra and into Marin. From there we can continue on into Vigo."

"Very good."

So north to Grove they traveled. The day was perfect weather-wise, and the scenery was utterly fantastic. Out beside the Atlantic Ocean they sped. The beaches were beautiful as the coastline twisted and turned into a large peninsula. There were many tourists, and each beach they passed was very crowded. They finally arrived in La Toja, an island resort, just off the coast from the town of Grove. Byrd parked the car, grabbed his beach hat, and opened the trunk to get Carmen's walking shoes.

"Come on, Luci. What's taking you so long?"

"I change clothes."

"In the car?"

"Si. You wait there."

After Luci had changed her clothes, the trio began their walk. The island was beautiful but very small. Trees abounded everywhere. There were raspberries, many flowers, and palm trees, too.

"What are all those people doing in the water? There are so many."

"I don't know. Maybe they are crabbing, or maybe they are digging for clams. I really don't know."

"We not know either."

They passed a gambling casino, a three-star and a five-star hotel, many local vendors, and a church constructed with a veneer to make it seem it was made from seashells. They arrived at the car again and drove over to Grove to eat.

The café they chose was unique: It specialized in seafood. So seafood was ordered: squid and spiced octopus! Byrd had never eaten octopus before, but he tasted it because he was hungry.

"How do you like it?" asked Carmen.

"It's different," Byrd replied, "but I like it."

"I don't believe you!" exclaimed Luci.

"Why?"

"You will eat anything we do. Most Americans do not do that. They are very particular."

"It must be shades of Thailand. There, you never asked about what you were eating. You just tasted what was served, and if it tasted good, you ate it! No questions asked."

"You surprise me."

"Peter Pan never surprises anyone. He just gives people what they really wish for."

"Is true."

They quickly finished the meal, and again drove south through Pontvedra into Marin. It only took thirty minutes.

"I don't like this place, either," said Carmen. "We leave."

They never stopped in Marin but continued south into Vigo. "Do you want to stop here?"

"There is that church over there on the hill. We could drive up to it and look at the city from there. I don't want to drive down into the main city."

"Is a good idea."

Byrd turned off the autopista and began to drive in the general direction of the church—or the hill—whichever was easier to see. He went down many narrow streets and only had his intuition to guide him. There were no sign posts.

"Oops, wrong way."

Back around the corner a right turn, and...

"Whee, we are here!"

"Ooh, is beautiful."

"Super!"

The hill overlooked the entire city, port, and bay of Vigo. The city was to the left—it was very, very large. The port and harbor lay in the center. There were many little boats afloat and one big oil freighter. To the right lay low hills scattered with houses. The blue sky, calm ocean. And serene atmosphere made the stop even more memorable. Byrd snapped many photographs here.

They finished the sightseeing and returned to the car. The road led to Orense, eastward, for the first time! Zaragoza was only five hundred kilometers away! The drive was hard, but the road was good. There were many hills and more than enough curves in the road. For the first time in their trip, the landscape changed dramatically. The hills became more prominent, and many of the trees disappeared. The vegetation scattered, and the general surrounding areas became drier. Two hours later, they arrived in Orense. Byrd was extremely tired.

Orense was a large city. It too was a provincial capital. Our travelers entered the city. They always chose that section because that is where all the shopping was located. Carmen and Luci loved to shop, and they would not have wanted it any other way! Byrd wound his way through a central business district. He turned into a side street which led to a church.

"Stop. Here is a spot."

"Great."

Parked, the three walked around the corner and down a short street. This led them straight to a two-star hotel!

"Look at this! What luck."

"We look in here."

"Si. Hay camas."

"Un doble y una primer, por favor."

"No problemo!"

They took the elevator up to their respective rooms.

"Look at this room! I'm in love!"

"Is beautiful."

"And look at all the furniture! A couch, two chairs, a coffee table, lamps, and, last but not least, a huge bathroom. I love it!"

"The beds are very big, too!"

Kisses and hugs! Kisses and hugs!

All of them met in the lobby later. Soon they were off exploring. They passed many shop windows. But the items displayed in them were not as nice as the girls had seen previously in other cities. The items were, however, just as expensive.

They ate at a two-fork restaurant for dinner. As they walked into the bar at the front, only a handful of people were present, and the volume of the television set was turned up so it could be heard throughout all parts of the bar, including the restaurant in the back! They proceeded on to the restaurant. Out of twenty set-up tables for customers, only one was occupied, and that by only two people.

"This must be a great place to eat," Byrd sarcastically stated, "with all the customers present! I'll bet the food is tremendous!"

"Maybe the food is good," Luci yelled over the din of the television. "No matter; I am very hungry."

"Nana is always hungry!" shouted Byrd.

They seated themselves at one of the empty tables. They chose fish, soup, a salad, and a fish stew for their dinners. All ordered agua sin gas to drink.

Time passed. Only the water and the ever-present bread were brought.

"Where is our food?" Luci sighed. "I think I am looking for my stomach again!"

"Why can't they turn down the television set?" asked Carmen to Byrd. "Is very noisy."

"Maybe they want us to hear it, too!" replied Byrd. "After all, this is a Two Fork establishment!"

"Turkey!" Carmen retorted to Byrd. Everyone laughed.

The waiter eventually brought their meals. The food really was good—and tasty, too! All in all, things weren't so bad except for the noise coming from the television set. After they had eaten and paid the bill, they again wandered along the streets looking at the costumes, jewelry, and shoes. More exploring. Their walk took them into a rundown area of the city. Cloistered streets, dirty dogs, and maimed people were prevalent. The area resembled the Tubes in downtown Zaragoza: good eating places, a street crowded with people, but absolutely atrocious surroundings. It was a real ghetto.

It was very dark by this time. The group retraced their steps and eventually arrived at their hotel. It was a welcome sight; each pair of feet was extremely tired. Byrd's right leg was hurting terribly from all the driving he had done. Neither of the girls wanted to drive, so Byrd had to do all of it. Pain! Pain!

A full stomach and a hot shower made each individual feel refreshed and sleepy. The rooms were a true delight, and the beds felt marvelous. Hugs and kisses! Kisses and hugs! Goodnight! (Friday, 21 August).

"Hi, Luci."

"Buenos dias. Buenos dias, Carmen."

"Buenos dias."

"Did you sleep well?"

"Yes, very good thank you. And you?"

"Like babies."

"Is good."

They loaded the car again, walked down the street, and ate a little breakfast. On their return to the car, Byrd spotted some Pazo in a store window.

"Look, Luci! Here's the wine you wanted to buy."

"Oh, good. I buy a few as presents for Christmas in Zaragoza."

Luci bought a few bottles of wine, alright—just twelve bottles!

"I thought you said you were only going to buy a few," Byrd stated.

"I do only buy a few," Luci replied.

"But twelve is just not a few. Twelve is many."

"I have many friends."

"I don't think I should have even entered this conversation. My mother always told me to never argue with a woman."

"Your mother was very smart."

They completed their brief shopping tour and continued on their journey. Eastward they traveled toward Leon. Carmen had again telephoned her brother, Javier, in Leon, to tell him when we would be there. He told her reservations had been made for the group in the Hotel Riosol. At least they would not have to worry about sleeping quarters as they did on their way to Oviedo.

The road to Leon was not the best. The curves were atrocious, and Byrd believed at times that he would drive into the rear of his own car because of all the turnouts, arcs, and otherwise doubled-back macadam, wiggles! They arrived in Ponferrada in mid-afternoon with little problem. They quickly found a small restaurant and ate a nice lunch. Once again in the car, they drove toward Leon.

The countryside quickly changed from dry, scantily covered hills and mountains to that of rather flat wheat lands. Compared to the mountains, it was vastly different, but the beauty that was displayed was a welcome change. In its own way, the land was picturesque. They turned off the main thoroughfare at Astorga and drove straight for Leon. The road was in excellent condition. And very straight, so time and kilometers sped quickly. The trio was in Leon before they realized it.

"Where to, Carmen?"

"La Hotel Riosol."

"Okay.'

They drove toward the city center, but due to a wrong turn, Byrd went around the western side and entered Leon from there. There was little traffic, and the signs were easily readable.

"What did you say the name of the hotel was, Carmen?"

"La Hotel Riosol."

"Okay.'

"Is this it?"

"Doh, si. Very good!"

Byrd parked the car around the corner from the hotel. Each carried his own luggage. They checked into the hotel; then they prepared themselves to meet Javier. Their toiletries completed, they walked next door to a bar to wait. Cold, non-alcoholic drinks were ordered because it was a hot day, and they had driven many kilometers. Alcohol would have been too much to handle.

Byrd watched the people cross the street as he looked out the window of the bar. It was a very beautiful day, and his seat proved to be an excellent vantage point. He spied a couple crossing the street with a little girl who was dressed in a completely red outfit. Byrd had met Carmen's sister and brother-in-law the day prior to the start of this vacation. The woman crossing the street seemed to be quite similar to Carmen's sister, Byrd mused. Oh, my God! It was Javier!

"Ooh eeh!" Carmen screamed as she ran to greet her relatives. Luci knew them too so she was equally excited. Byrd casually followed.

"Javier, this is our friend, Byrd," introduced Carmen.

"Buenos."

"Byrd, this is my brother, Javier; his wife, Maria Jesus; and my niece, Elena."

"Hola."

Everyone walked over to Javier's little Seat. Javier and Byrd sat up front, and all the others were packed into the rear seat. Javier first drove them to the new apartment he had just bought.

The apartment was beautifully big and beautifully furnished. It consisted of two, large bedrooms, a very large kitchen, and many smaller enclaves. Byrd immediately liked it.

"Would you three like something to drink?" Javier asked.

"Si. Agua, agua, Coca-Cola."

"Muy bien."

The refreshments tasted good for it had already been a tiring morning.

"Are you hungry?"

"Un poco."

Maria Jesus served all kinds of snacks: assorted nuts, cheeses, and various kinds of crackers. Most of the snacks were consumed by the travelers. Little did they realize that this was only the appetizer for all the food to come later.

After all had been refreshed, Javier wanted to show the trio the city of Leon. He would act as personal guide. Down to the car and into the city they traveled. First he drove them past the main plaza. It was characterized by a large and very beautiful water fountain. Leon's main attraction, however, was the cathedral. That is where they traveled to next.

The cathedral was a beautiful Gothic, thirteenth-century structure. It had two, large spires in the front. The main door was made of hand-carved figures etched in wood. It was quite exquisite. Inside, the entire building was framed innumerable stained-glass windows. A huge, rose window of many colors adorned the front just above the main doorway. Byrd was too enthralled with looking at all the windows to take pictures or to remember much else.

They next went to a small church where a mass was being held. No time was spent in the mass, however. The church, though, was very big and very beautiful. From the church, they walked to the restaurant where Javier had made dinner reservations for the evening. More window shopping followed. As evening approached, everyone walked toward the five-star hotel of San Martins. It was on old monastery converted into a three-hundred room hotel! It was very plush; it was also very expensive. The main lounge was serene and comfortable. Drinks were ordered, and more snacks (this time peanuts) were eaten. Javier paid for all the drinks. Guests were guests, no matter where one traveled.

It was finally time for dinner. The group left San Martins, took Elena home, and then went to where Javier had made dinner reservations. The restaurant itself was located in a small, crowded basement of a rather large building. A table for five had been reserved in one corner. That was good because all the other seats were occupied. It was a very popular eating establishment in Leon. Bread and wine were served first. All orders were given to the waiter, and everyone had much to discuss in the meantime. The conversations were all in Spanish (as were most throughout the entire trip), so Byrd did not understand much. Carmen translated when necessary but, otherwise, Byrd just watched all the people and drank his wine. The salads were served first. Byrd ordered a giant bowl of raw shrimp mixed with herbs, spices, and a sauce. Luci and Carmen ate fish soup. Byrd could not finish the entire bowl; he had too much previously, and there was just too much. Carmen and Luci did the same. The main course was then brought: steak, a lettuce salad, and French-fried potatoes on an eighteen-inch diameter plate!

"Oh, God, no more food," Byrd groaned.

Carmen and Luci were also astounded. Byrd slowly ate his steak and salad. He didn't have the heart to touch the French fries! He managed to eat the entire steak and all the salad. The girls barely touched anything on their plates, they were so full. Most of the French fries and the bread were left uneaten by practically everyone. Diets were definitely not on the menu that day!

The time was now past midnight. The bill for the dinners arrived, and again Javier paid everything! Byrd was very upset at this, but no one seemed to notice. It was all part of the evening. All five people rolled out of the restaurant; they could barely walk because of all the food they had consumed. Javier drove them around the corner to a cocktail lounge for after-dinner drinks.

"More food?" Byrd complained.

"No, just drinks," reassured Carmen.

"Hooray! I don't think I'll be able to eat for a week. I'm stuffed!"

"You look it!" laughed Carmen.

"Thanks. I needed that!" retorted Byrd. "Turkey!"

"Don't call me turkey!"

"Okay neighbor."

"Is better."

Byrd drank an Irish coffee, his first in Spain, and it was quite good. The girls each ordered manzanilla (apple juice). Javier drank Scotch. Light and jovial conversation abounded, but the length of the day and all the activity finally prevailed. Everyone was visibly tired.

"We go now."

This time, however, Byrd paid the bill. "I'm awfully tired."

"I, too."

Javier drove the three back to the Hotel Riosol.

"Muchas gracias, Javier, para todos," Byrd exclaimed in his very limited Spanish.

"Mucho gusto," Javier replied.

Hands were shaken, and kisses were given.

"Buenos noches."

"Buenos noches."

Back at the hotel, it was, "Goodnight, Carmen," "Good night, neighbor." Zzzz. (Saturday, 22 August)

At ten o'clock the next morning, the trio was once again eating croissants and drinking café con leche. After breakfast they began to window shop. Byrd wanted to see the cathedral again so they ventured in that direction.

They arrived at the cathedral but did not enter. Byrd took more pictures as they walked. After walking around the cathedral, they walked to the church they had entered during the mass celebration. The small museum in it was open so they explored what it offered. One room had a gallery of illuminated photographs. Each picture displayed represented a different monastery somewhere in Spain. All the photographs were black and white, and this made them starker in their realism. They were professionally done, and all were done well.

After the tour of the museum and the church, the three made their way back to the car. They drove south out of Leon past flat farmlands of wheat. Forty kilometers later, Byrd turned off the main road and began an easterly drive that would take them into Burgos and eventually home.

"What are you doing back there, Luci? Byrd asked. "Cooling off."

As Byrd looked in the rear to where Luci sat, he asked, "How are you doing that? The windows are already open."

"Do not look!" screamed Luci. "I am not dressed!"

"Oh, I can see that!"

Luci had removed her jogging pants while they sped through the hot, dry, dusty country. She had them draped across her legs but, otherwise, she was nude from the waist down, excluding her panties, of course. Damn! She was comfortable, and there was no one to see them in all the desolate countryside. It did not bother Byrd or Carmen in the least.

The wheat fields quickly disappeared. The terrain was still occasionally flat, but now only rocks, dust, and prairie predominated. Three hours later Byrd drove the car into Burgos.

They entered the central parking area. Since it was Sunday, traffic and people were non-existent. Byrd parked the car. They walked across an empty plaza. The only movement anywhere was the pigeons flying around the plaza as the trio walked through them. They window shopped a little, but they were not very interested today. Their main reason for stopping in Burgos was to visit the cathedral there also.

The cathedral in Burgos was quite different than the one in Leon. It was constructed between the thirteenth and fourteenth centuries. Its facade also contained two steeples, but the structure between then was vastly different from Leon's, inside, there was only one stained-glass window. The main attraction for Byrd, however, was five huge sculpted marble murals. Each mural displayed some aspect of Christ's life. Though very different, they too were awe-inspiring.

After the visit, it was again time to eat. They stopped at a little outside café that was open. They ordered beef, salads, and lamb.

By this time, everyone was drinking agua sin gas. Beer or wine were not very desirable drinks for any of them on this entire trip. The day was warm and sunny, and this made the lunch much nicer. They prolonged the respite as long as possible. None of the three really wanted to begin traveling again. The trip was getting tiresome for them all.

"Are you ready to go, Byrd?" Carmen asked.

"No, not really. Are you?"

"Si."

"Do you want to drive?"

"No."

"Okay," Byrd replied. He really did wish that Carmen would drive; his left leg was becoming more and more cramped as the kilometers passed. Four more hours of non-stop driving would almost cripple him for three days. Walking helped, but in bed at night, the pain was unbearable at times.

Shouldering the load, Byrd once again walked to the car. East. Click, click, click. Across desolate landscape. Past the two thousand kilometer mark. Most places were dry, dusty, and uninhabited. Two hours later, they finally got onto the autopista near Logrono. Click, click, click. Past Logrono and on toward Tudela. The closer they drove to Zaragoza, the drier the surroundings became. Dust clouds hung like dark blankets in the air. "Of all the traveling we've done in the last eight days." Byrd thought to himself. "Zaragoza is the worst area we've seen. And we live there!" Ugh, how depressing.

Click, click, click. Past Tudela and Luci's home they drove. Luci said she did not want to stop; she would be there next weekend anyway. She did tell Byrd about some of the sights there and about the church. Byrd made a mental note to himself to drive to Tudela some Sunday to look at the town and to take some pictures there.

Soon all three began to see signs familiar to them. Zaragoza loomed on the horizon. No one spoke. Maybe it was because everyone was tired; maybe it was because the truly happy trip was nearing an end. If anyone knew the real reason, no one wanted to express it. No one wanted to break the magical spell. All were quiet. Only the sound of the car's engine was heard. Thoughts were scattered, but they were not far from each other. They were together—just as Peter Pan, Wendy, and Nana were together for a short while in Never-Never Land.

They soon entered the Zaragoza city limits. Byrd drove directly to Luci's apartment. Byrd parked out front and unloaded all her luggage, including the twelve bottles of Pazo wine.

"Good-bye, Luci," Byrd said.

"Adios," Luci responded as she kissed him on both cheeks in the European custom. "You are very fun to travel with. Thank you very much. Adios, Carmen. Hasta manana."

"Adios, Luci."

"Good-bye again."

Byrd returned to the car and slowly drove through Zaragoza. Carmen's apartment was on the other side of town so it took him awhile to wend his way through all the traffic. It was not like Burgos in the least! Carmen's parents were not home; they had gone to the resort town of Benicasin and vacation while Carmen was on her trip.

"Will you come to pick me up later?" asked Carmen.

"Sure," stated Byrd. "What time?"

"Is ten o'clock fine?"

"It's fine."

"Muy bien. See you at ten!"

The time was currently past eight. Byrd quickly drove to the air base, collected his mail, and drove home. He rearranged all his bags once he got back to the apartment, unpacked clothes, and opened packages. After a quick shower and shave, he returned to the car and drove across town to get Carmen.

"Hola."

"Hi, love." A quick kiss. "Where do you want to go?"

"We go to your place. Is very lonely and sad at home. I iron your shirts."

"Okay."

Later, Carmen was ironing Byrd's shirts while he read his mail and wrote checks. Even though he had been gone for more than a week, he did not have very much mail to answer. He had no bills to pay either!

"My parents called while I was home," stated Carmen. "They were checking on me. I don't like that. Luci and I will see them tomorrow when we drive down to Benicasim. I tell them about the vacation."

"Don't worry about it," Byrd replied. "They do it because they love you. My parents do the same thing to me whenever I'm home. After all, you are the baby of the family!"

"Is true, but I am a grown woman now."

"I know. I can definitely see that! Don't let it bother you. My parents do the same thing to me whenever I'm home on leave, or if I've traveled anywhere. It's just natural."

"Do you have some white wine open?"

"No, but I will."

Byrd went to get each of them a glass of wine while Carmen continued her ironing.

"Ooh, is good. Thank you very much."

"You know you don't have to iron my shirts. They really don't need it."

"I know I don't have to iron your shirts, but I want to do it. And yes, they do need ironed. They look better ironed."

"Okay, if you say so."

A little while later, Carmen finished. It was now past midnight.

"I'm tired, Carmen. I can barely stay awake. My leg is killing me."

"I'm tired too. Let's go to bed."

Together they walked into the bedroom, undressed, and crawled beneath the lone sheet. The night was very warm. Both were completely exhausted.

"Good night, love. This is a vacation I will never forget. It truly was a trip to Never-Never Land.

A quiet kiss. A gentle hug. Good night.

(Sunday, 23 August)

CPSIA information can be obtained
at www.ICGtesting.com
Printed in the USA
BVHW041821060322
630768BV00014B/990